SEEKER of FREEDOM and JOY

Inspiring life journeys of an enlightened heart

DEBRA A. LANSDOWNE

Seeker of Freedom and Joy

An Inspiring life journey of an enlightened heart.

Copyright © 2019 by Debra A Lansdowne

All rights reserved.

No part of this book may be reproduced in any form or by any electronic or mechanical means including information storage and retrieval systems, without permission in writing from the author. The only exception is by a reviewer, who may quote short excerpts in a review.

Published by: Sojourn Publishing, LLC

Published for: Debra A Lansdowne (aka Debra Lansdowne)

Book and Cover designed by JetLaunch

in collaboration with the Author

Author Photo back cover by Photographer Sandy Black

Author website www.Heartjourneyswithdebra.com

Email: heartjourneys006@gmail.com

The events and stories in this book are all true as the author remembers them but the names have been changed to protect the privacy of those involved.

Distributed in paperback and electronic forms.

Paperback IBSN: 978-1-64184-247-1
Ebook ISBN: 978-1-64184-248-8

In loving memory of my dad,
Kevin Henry Lansdowne, and my Ancestors.

Contents

Acknowledgements vii
Introduction ix

1	Dad's Advocate	1
2	Dad's Gift	10
3	Shadows with Hidden Gems	19
4	The Family Sponge	26
5	Generational Trauma	40
6	Potato Chips and Friday Nights	47
7	I Love You	58
8	The Caged Lion	72
9	Culture and Curiosity	83
10	Dogs and Me	86
11	Heart Calling	98
12	True to My Nature	114
13	Dreams Happen	124
14	Body Wisdom and Intelligence	142
15	Grief: Nowhere to Hide	154
16	Epiphany and Revelations	167

17	Secrets Come Out	177
18	Awakened and Conscious Now	185
19	A UFO?	196
20	A Force of Nature	204
21	Unexpected Message	210
22	Other Realms	220
23	My Ancestors	232
24	Child of Mother Earth	249
25	Biological Earth Battery	265
26	Don't Forget the Animals	272
27	My Soul Knows the Way	281
28	My Heart Tells Me Every Day	295

References 305
About the Author 307

Acknowledgements

This book is dedicated to my father, for his love and encouragement to share my gifts by writing this book, and to my mother, for birthing me onto the planet and being my tough love advocate to help me see my strengths.

I thank my sister, Kim, for her love and for sharing her extraordinary healing knowledge.

I give gratitude to Nigel, my husband, who is extraordinary and accepts an empowered woman. Thank you, Nigel, for your unconditional love and support during our incredible life as travellers of many worlds.

I am also grateful to:

Mother Earth, who has always been there for me and continues to remind me I am loved, and that I hold a strong passion and love inside of me for this planet and all beings.

All the beautiful wise souls who have come into my life in different animal forms to support me.

My ancestors, for their loving support and for reminding me I am not alone; they are walking with me in love beyond this 3D reality.

The many teachers who have crossed my life path, in joyful times and as my advocates to challenge me, to see with my spiritual eyes of consciousness.

My writing mentor, Tom Bird, for his guidance and encouragement to find my divine author within.

And last but not least, a beautiful heart and talented editor, Karen Collyer, for using her magic to make my manuscript into this wonderful book that you can now read with ease. Such gratitude to have Karen and Tom to support my author journey.

Introduction

I wrote this book for me, but mostly for you.

We are all brothers and sisters, divine sparks looking to find our way joyfully back to the ocean of consciousness, light and love.

Your soul wants to help you find purpose and passion, to have the joy of magic unfold in your life, to give you amazing and unbelievable experiences beyond your mind's limited thinking.

This book is a road map, with landmarks shared transparently to show how my heart and soul guided me to a more conscious life, one filled with freedom, joy and love. I offer this to inspire you to find your own path beyond the challenges and fears we all struggle with in life.

Take this road map, use it to identify the landmarks as you explore, and satisfy your desire to find greater freedom, love and Joy.

If you can go beyond the fear of what it takes to do the journey, you'll find it is a life journey, not an overnight quick fix, as it takes time and much compassion for yourself. You are then able to offer compassion to others, and by leaving judgment behind, you can find a way forward to freedom and empowerment by using your own resources and wisdom.

Whatever your situation, the resources required are within you, so look past the moment you are experiencing. Know that what challenges you now have will pass. You will find the strength from this experience to move forward, to see the message that is trying to be heard or be seen for your own enlightenment.

Look past the personal and you will find your way. Go into your heart and allow your heart and soul to guide you; bypass the mind of judgment that will control you and cause you to miss the joy that awaits you.

"Your vision will become clear, only when you look into your heart. Who looks outside, dreams. Who looks inside, awakens."

Carl Gustav Jung

I write as a soul who has explored the heart and emotions — a challenging path at times, with much emotional and physical pain. My heart has been broken open, closed down, and opened again to find greater love. Through my own resistance, healing, and many transformations, I navigated my way through the heart to find my freedom. With freedom I discovered my own empowerment, allowing wisdom, joy, love, abundance, and magic into my life.

While life has taken me on many journeys, I never had a plan. Life just unfolded, and as I trusted my own inner guidance, it started to heal the shadows in my heart. This expanded my heart to find a new awareness and new realities beyond this 3D world of illusion, to journey with Mother Earth and our ancestors.

SEEKER of FREEDOM and JOY

This book has lived inside my heart for some time, and has grown into the force of a lion, roaring at me to let it out.
That force is my soul.

1

Dad's Advocate

What I remember most about my dad are his bright, clear, sky-blue eyes.

How those eyes smiled at me! I could feel his soul smiling back at me, his heart embracing mine. Dad had a strength about him, an inner force I could feel around him, filled with love. He was full of fun, humour, and knew what freedom felt like, as he enjoyed being in the great outdoors with nature. I remember him as the heart of our home in the early days, and I adored him.

Then an event in his life changed him, and us, irrevocably.

Have you ever seen a loved one struggle for their life?
How did that feel for you?

It can be daunting, scary to watch, or a blessing and honour to be present with a loved one as they move on and change form.

We do not talk about death enough in Western society, unlike many ancient and indigenous cultures who celebrate and accept death as part of life. We struggle, even though death is what we are all moving toward every day. It does not matter your age or race — we are all equal in the eyes of death when it is time to leave Mother Earth.

I remember my first experience of death. As a trainee nurse of only two months' experience, I was placed on a ward where an elderly patient had just died. I was instructed to help a senior nurse lay the poor lady out. When we moved the patient onto her side, the last air in her lungs came bursting out in a huge sigh. This sent me into hysterical laughter, and I had to be taken outside the ward to settle down.

It was not that I was being disrespectful, I just had not seen a dead person before. My mind went into overload, unconsciously sending me into an almighty laugh. I realised later it was my coping mechanism. I had used it before — in my school years in situations to which I did not know how to react. Some fifteen years later in my nursing career I had seen a good deal of death, but I was about to experience it from an entirely new perspective — watching death from a very personal and emotional connection, of a loved one I knew well.

I watched my father struggle for his life in a hospital bed, while his spirit was slipping away from his body. This became one of those extremely challenging journeys life throws at you, forcing you to look at your own mortality and make some really big changes in your life. For me, that involved transforming into a new version of myself, to find answers to those life questions of who am I really and why am I here? This does not happen in a hurry. It takes time and trusting your own inner compass — our heart — to guide you.

My Dad at fifty-five years of age had been suffering for twenty years with Alpha-1 Antitrypsin deficiency (A1AD), a severe lung disease. There was no cure, and he was getting progressively worse. A1AD is due to a protein enzyme deficiency in the blood. It affects the lungs and/or liver and allows the lungs to be damaged by air pollution and smoking. The symptoms are similar too Congestive Obstructive Pulmonary Disease (COPD): shortness of breath, wheezing, chronic coughs, lots of sputum, recurring colds and pneumonia, allergies, and low tolerance to exercise.

Basically, Dad could not breathe normally. He struggled to get air in and out of his lungs and was at high risk for lung infections. From its onset, the condition was a slow decline into poor health and would eventually take his life. To this day, no cure has been found.

A1AD is a genetic condition. My father's family carries the genes, and my grandfather died of the same disease after he had a serious motor-vehicle accident while working as a fireman.

There was not much known about A1AD then, nor is there now. Apparently, it had been dormant in my father's body, so he experienced no symptoms and did not know it had been passed on to him. A serious car accident in his early thirties caused dangerous injuries, including broken ribs that punctured and collapsed Dad's lungs, shocking his body system and activating A1AD.

Dad spent the next twenty years in and out of hospital with lung infections, struggling to breathe. In his late forties, Dad reluctantly surrendered to using an oxygen cylinder, as he could not push himself any longer to get oxygen into his lungs. In the later years, leading up to the lung transplant, doctors would regularly say on hospital admissions, "He may not make it this time." Dad always proved them wrong, as he had such a strong will and determination to live. I wonder if I got that stubborn determination from Dad's genes?

In 1990, aged fifty-five, Dad was offered a place on the lung transplant list by Dr. Chan, a specialist heart/lung surgeon. Dad agreed to the operation if they could find a donor. They did, and in 1991 Dad became the first man in Australia to have a lung transplant.

When the call came, Mum and Dad had moved just three days earlier to a new house purpose-built for Dad's condition. It overlooked the north coast beaches, only ninety minutes from Sydney. Ironically, the land was paid for by the small compensation Dad had received twenty years earlier for the motor-car accident which had caused A1AD to be activated. Dad was told to go straight to the hospital; if he was a match with the donor (a middle-aged woman who had just died in a car accident) they would operate immediately. Dad was lucky to find a donor so quickly.

On the day of the transplant, we were taken to the visitors' room where we would wait for many hours, not knowing if Dad would survive the operation — he was a test case, as the first man in Australia to have a lung transplant. When Dad was being anaesthetised, Dr. Chan came out to let us know he would not be doing two lung transplants, he had changed his mind and would now only be transplanting one lung, Dad's other lung would be left in place.

We were surprised to receive this comment from the doctors, and it seeded some doubt in our minds for Dad's success. Later, we were told the change in plans gave Dad a better chance to recover. Dad came through the operation, and we could all breathe again, I say in jest. It was a long operation and many hours had passed before we were told it was successful.

Dad spent time in an Intensive Care Unit, and later moved to a rehabilitation ward for activities and monitoring before he went home. The doctors were really pleased with his progress and stated how he had exceeded their expectations. What were they expecting? I did not ask, we were just glad to have him back. Dad's strength kept him going through all sorts of challenges; he just never gave up.

Finally, Dad went home to enjoy the new lung and freedom from the oxygen cylinder! However, he still had to go to the hospital for frequent check-ups and drug adjustments. What made him happy was a small sense of freedom returning. Little activities, like walking to the local shop to get the newspaper, had not been possible before the transplant. After, he could enjoy a slow walk to the shop, giving him a wonderful sense of achievement. We were privileged to see the biggest smile on his face when he walked, taking his two-year-old granddaughter with him.

Something my father shared with our family, which intrigued me at the time, was that he was experiencing the old memories from the donor's lung. He would say he was getting memories from incidents that were not part of his life previously, as a female. He was certain they were memories held in the lung he had received.

Twenty-seven years on, I know it is highly possible he was picking up on the memories of the donor lung at a cellular level. This is what I have learnt and experienced through therapy trainings — trauma memories are actually held in the body, so healing the body through conscious movement therapy can release the memory. Dad also had a sense of the donor around him, energetically. He could not explain it; it was more of a knowing.

I know from living in an Australian Aboriginal community that they are very keen to take all the belongings of a person who has died to be burned, so the person can be released and not held back spiritually on this earthly plane.

Maybe this opens up a whole new cultural discussion around organ transplants?

Do you know of anyone who has shared similar feelings from an organ transplant? When Dad talked about it, I had not heard this before, or at least not anyone admitting to having these feelings after a transplant.
I had a lot to learn!

Sadly, almost twelve months to the day after Dad received the lung transplant, he acquired a severe cold in his old lung. This quickly turned into pneumonia, due to his very low immunity from being on immune-suppressant drugs. Dad was taken to hospital and his body rapidly turned from serious infection to septic (full body infection). After six weeks of struggling to stay alive, Dad's body slowly shut down, causing kidney failure. I was there every day and watched him struggle and lose his strength, going steadily downhill.

The doctors thought Dad would be a good candidate for the lung transplant because his other organs were very strong, but his time to leave this life was closing in on him. Unfortunately, on his last admission to hospital with pneumonia, his body had already gone through so much with the lung transplant and heavy medications that he could not fight the infection any longer.

It changed my life to see him go through that horrible, painful experience over six weeks. He had always been a proud and very private man who looked after himself with great dignity. To be at the mercy of hospital staff, bathing, and toileting him in bed, would have been very upsetting for him.

Dad had really suffered, but always said, "It will help science, even if it is not successful for me." My mum, sister, and I had not been all that keen for him to have a transplant. From my previous nursing experience, I knew the road would be challenging. But we all wanted to support his decision, his need to feel freedom — without the oxygen cylinder. He shared with me one day, "Maybe I will play golf again, Deb." I just smiled. I could not dampen his hope.

One morning, leading up to the day he left his physical body, I remember especially well. I arrived to find him bombed out on many drugs. Approaching, I saw him have an involuntary full-body shaking fit, something he had never suffered from before. I felt helpless. What was going on?

My heart broke, feeling his discomfort and the lack of privacy with all the medical team around his bed. Was Dad ever going to have peace? That was it for me — I had to do something. I needed to be dad's advocate. I was ready to battle with the doctors for Dad's peace. It was time to tap into my old nursing experience and assertively get to the bottom of this bizarre event my father had suffered.

My gut feeling said something was amiss. Confronting the doctors, I eventually found out they were not communicating with one another and had given him two drugs that were contraindicated and not compatible, causing him to have seizures. That was insane! His whole body was already struggling to keep the infection under control, this made me so angry.

The specialist doctor was not there, but when he arrived the next morning, I cornered him in the corridor with his entourage of medical specialists, residents, and registrars.

"If that was your father dying in that bed, would you be giving all these drugs? What good are you doing? You know he is dying you have told us. Please let him die in peace with just pain relief," I implored.

The doctors heard me and had a meeting, resulting in only one specialist being responsible for Dad's medical treatment instead of a group of specialists who were not working as a team. The problem was, each specialist had focused only on their own speciality body system, prescribing medications without consulting with the other specialists, thus causing my father's seizure event.

I did not know until my mother told me later, but when Dad was offered the transplant my parents had signed many papers. They had agreed for the doctors to basically do what they liked to his body — it would no longer be his body it was now seen as research. I am glad I did not know that at the time!

After my confrontation with the medical team they suggested my mother, sister, and I go for counselling with the chaplain. Why? To soothe their own guilt? We were not deluded in our attempts to help Dad find peace in his last days. Specialist doctors are not used to families speaking up and questioning their actions. Of course we were stressed, who wouldn't be under the circumstances? But I was not going to stop making those doctors accountable for their actions, and I kept watching over my dad.

This I feel is the problem with our medical system — doctors do not see the whole person in the bed. In comparison, in complementary therapies the whole person is seen and treated in an integrated approach with the patient. I have seen the medical model cause patients so much harm with treatments, and now I was witnessing my father in the same position.

On the day of my thirty-third birthday at 11 am, my father passed away. It was 1991, the year I will not forget. He was fifty-six years old.

2

Dad's Gift

The last six weeks of Dad's life brought up many emotions for me. I knew he wanted to die at home, so I offered to care for him, but Mum did not feel she could cope. I felt so sad that he did not get his wish.

Mum and I were present at the time of Dad's passing. My sister was late, as she'd had a very sick child turn up at her natural-health practice two hours away, so missed him on the hour of passing.

I noticed that after passing Dad did not leave the room. I had my hand on his head, saying, "It's okay Dad, you can go and find peace now, we will be okay. I will look after Mum for you."

Mum was standing anxiously on the other side of the bed. The church minister was talking to her, having just given Dad a blessing, moments before I watched my father take his last breath.

I know Dad felt very guilty for leaving Mum, because he told me so. He had always felt he was her saviour, by taking her away from the foster family home where she had lived through her childhood and teen years. Mum and Dad were married quite young; Mum was nineteen, and Dad twenty-one. They met at

Dad's sister's wedding. Dad said he knew that day that he would marry my mum. The day after the meeting, he began sending her love letters and travelled long distances on public transport to court her. Somewhat romantic, as Mum remembers. I remember how much they did love one another most of the time.

Mum was holding Dad when he died. He was looking at her and he was so loving. I had my hand at the top of his head as he took his last breath. In that moment, I felt his spirit go out of the crown of his head. I say this because it felt like a breeze had passed my hand. A very strange feeling, but very real. My own body had strange feelings I had never experienced before.

I felt a little disappointed, as Dad did not acknowledge me when he passed over. I remember I wanted to play my compact disc with opera singing before Dad passed, but the minister and Mum abruptly said, "Turn that off." I was so upset, I knew how Dad loved opera and classical music; he just loved all music.

Then something strange happened.

The minister, hospital staff, Mum, and I were standing around the bed, acknowledging that Dad had died. Then the staff and minister all turned away, with their backs toward Dad's bed, and started talking to Mum. I continued to watch my dad.

Suddenly, Dad opened his eyes and returned to his body. What was going on? He was looking for Mum, trying to get her attention with his eyes, but she was busy talking with the minister and had her head turned away.

"Mum! Look, please! Dad wants you," I called out.

As she looked over the bed at Dad a solitary teardrop rolled down his face. Looking at her lovingly, he said it all in that moment with those clear, sky-blue eyes. He loved her, and he was sorry for leaving her.

The staff witnessed this event too. They said they had, "... never seen such a dying moment," with a patient being clinically dead, then returning to his body and opening his eyes, with that deep, soulful look of love transmitted across the bed toward my mother. They all felt moved, as I did. I should not be surprised, for my family has never really fitted into the normal box. Although I had been a nurse for many years prior, I had never seen a dying moment like this before, either.

The other twist was that even after that moment with Mum, I knew Dad was still in the room. I could feel and sense his energy, up near the ceiling to one side of the room. I believe he stayed there until my sister arrived and was able to say good-bye, which she did about one hour later. After she said her good-bye, I felt him leave the room.

I don't remember ever sensing such strong feelings or psychic experiences around someone dying before that moment. It really woke me up to my psychic abilities. *I felt it was a gift to behold from my father, and I treasured being shown it.*

It opened my heart to be more conscious about the dying process. Many years later this experience helped me when I returned to nursing as a Specialist Palliative Care Nurse, working with families and supporting patients to pass over in a more conscious way, in their homes. It also helped me be consciously present with other beings, such as the animals I have helped to pass over in wildlife rescue.

It felt like an extraordinary and magical experience all at once, and it inspired me to want to know more about the other side of death and spirituality — which I'd had no interest in until that moment. Suddenly I was curious! From that day, I began an awesome spiritual journey to find out more about death. It also put me on a fast track to learn about esoteric sciences of the unseen world and spirituality, of which my sister had been learning and practicing in her clinic. Sometimes I was her test body, to try out vibrational healing techniques she was learning from a master healer.

So for me, my father's death was a blessing in disguise.

He inspired me to go on another journey, which I travel to this day. So much unfolded after Dad's passing. Another healing journey began — my life basically went into the pits, with my job becoming very stressful. I had not realised, or admitted, the full extent of my grief, so I worked hard to distract myself from dealing with the painful feelings and the emptiness inside.

My dad with the clear, sky-blue eyes was no longer on this plane of existence. I could not even feel him around me. I was numb, with a broken heart. It felt like part of my heart had been ripped away from me. Knowing that he was going to die, having time to prepare, did not lessen the intense pain in my heart.

≈

I remember my father, those bright eyes and the soulful smile that embraced me. I always felt his big heart holding me, and the strength that surrounded him. Dad was full of fun and adventure, loved his freedom, had a great sense of humour, and loved to socialise. As a father he was loving and giving, however I found him to be a man of limited conversation, as he was a deep thinker who kept his feelings to himself. He never shared opinions unless asked and would think carefully before responding. And he had conservative ideas about the roles of men and women in society.

Dad was physically very strong in his younger years, before his serious car accident, and loved his sports, playing or watching cricket, football, tennis, and swimming, that was until he was no longer able to play any sports.

Dad was the heart of our family. As a child I loved to spend time with him on our family outings and holidays. His love of the great outdoors gave us great school holidays to beautiful beach locations. I loved those holidays where he taught us to fish, swim, and play cricket. I always felt his sense of fun and adventure. I remember one holiday Dad wanted to go camping, but not with a caravan. Mum made it clear she was not going unless she had her comforts accommodated, like the kitchen sink and a proper bed, tent with walls and flooring - the list seemed endless. Mum has always been more of a homebody, a lover of the arts and live theatre shows, not so comfortable in the wild outdoors. During school holidays Mum would take us to see live theatre shows, opera, or children's pantomime.

In so many ways I remember my parents being opposite, but Dad loved to please my mother, and he was good at making things with his hands, so he welded steel frame beds for us all and made a kitchen sink, with all the extra places to put things. We even had fabric wall dividers to separate the bedroom spaces in the twelve-foot by twelve-foot marque canvas tent we owned in the 1960s. Dad was so excited to go camping; his challenge was to get Mum on board too.

Even though my parents weren't wealthy, Dad made things for us, and Mum created and made clothes for my sister and me. When we became teenagers, Mum showed us how to design and make our own fashionable creations to wear. Dad always seemed to get quite a sense of satisfaction out of making things around the house. One year he made my sister and I the best big dolls house, with two levels, front and back doors, rooms upstairs and down, painted all white with red trim. We loved it as our Christmas present.

The car accident that changed all our lives, but especially Dad's, was quite traumatic. Dad was driving home from a golf day with my two uncles. They were crossing an intersection when a young driver, speeding at around 80 kph, smashed into their car on the driver's side. Dad was rammed in the chest and my uncles both sustained serious injuries.

Dad's lungs were punctured and had collapsed, so he could barely breathe. Half unconscious, he wanted to know if my uncles were okay. Residents in nearby houses heard the noise and rushed to help. They tried to get Dad out of the car, but struggled and called the ambulance.

Dad said the pain he sustained when the locals tried to get him out was excruciating, causing him to black out. The ambulance rushed him to hospital, while police notified my mum and aunts, who had noticed the men were late returning but hadn't worried, as we were on holiday time together at a holiday house.

Mum rushed us all to hospital and I could not believe what I saw.

Only ten years old, I was so scared. My dad looked all tied up with intravenous lines, and a tube into his throat attached to a machine that was helping him to breathe. I don't remember him being conscious at that visit. I was devastated to see him like that, and the hospital staff were concerned for his condition, unsure if it would improve. A few days later, he was conscious and showing his strength to us all, but he was still looking in very poor shape, with intravenous tubes and bruises all over him.

Dad finally came home and had a few months off work. He received a small compensation but was forced to leave his job because he could not physically keep up. I think this really challenged him, as he had considered himself to be a good provider for his family. Now he had to consider another way to earn money. And he did, by going into the fencing business with my uncle, but it did not last. So again, he was challenged to find another job.

This time he decided to start his own car-restoration business, which he loved. Dad was a real craftsman at bringing cars back to new and reselling them. The local car dealers would look for his cars to buy, as he had a good reputation for quality workmanship. He may have loved the work and the satisfaction it offered him, but I feel it is what sped up the lung-disease process, because he had to use spray paints on the cars. Nowadays, we know that is definitely not a good occupation for anyone with a lung disorder.

Dad changed after his motor accident. He seemed to get very angry and frustrated with his life as he started to go to the hospital with lung problems. Unable to breathe adequately in the winter months, Dad acquired lung infections (bronchitis or pneumonia) and needed to be admitted for treatment. He was forced to use Ventolin inhalers every day, and did not like that restriction. His physical life had changed so much; he no longer had the stamina or energy to keep up his sport, so he let it go.

Our family felt the change too, as he would get quite angry very quickly, which through my child's eyes seemed to be for no real reason. His anger really showed up on one of our camping trips. We had gone shopping and left our dog tied up next to the tent for a few hours, on a tent peg. Big problem — our dog got bored and chewed the side of the tent, making a gaping hole. Wow, that dog nearly lost his life! Dad nearly killed him, hitting him in anger. I felt so sorry for our poor dog, he did not know what he had done.

Many years later, my sister and I believe my father may have been suffering with undiagnosed post-traumatic stress disorder (PTSD) after his motor-car accident. It was not picked up by anyone, as Dad would never have admitted having mental-health problems.

I believed the physical challenges with his lungs were all he could deal with, as men of his era (born in 1936) would not discuss their feelings. It would have been seen as a weakness.

≈

My insight here:
I feel blessed and honoured to have had the opportunity to be at my father's side as he passed from his body and this world, and for being shown my clairsentient and clairvoyant abilities.

My parents also showed me the power of love in the moment of dying (passing on to another place beyond this existence). Dad left me with a strong curiosity to learn about conscious dying and supporting other people and beings to die more consciously. My experience of Dad's death encouraged me to look at spirituality more deeply. Before his death, my interest was limited to astrology, numerology, and yoga.

Strange as this may sound, I also felt my father did not acknowledge me to say good-bye when he was dying. This gave me a strong need to find a way to communicate with him again, beyond this existence, like mediums and channels do when they talk to dead people. But I would have to learn more; thus my curiosity sent me on many a journey into the ancient earth mystery school teachings, esoteric sciences and spirituality.

Have you seen death? If so, did you ever find a deeper meaning behind this very deep emotional time in your life? Did you find any message or gift there for yourself?

3

Shadows with Hidden Gems

A sensitive child, I experienced the world through my heart. I started out a happy, optimistic, curious and loving child, who was keen to explore the world, until something changed at home. Suddenly, my small world contained pain and suffering, and life became very confusing as I tried to understand the new emotions in my heart. I remember my childhood became difficult after school age.

> *Have you ever felt the storm around you, or directed at you, when someone you love is deeply angry toward you? How did that feel for you?*

I adored my father. He was a central figure in my younger years before I left home. We had some heated moments over the years, but I could always feel his heart shining brightly toward me, even when he was angry with me. He could not hide what his heart and soul were reflecting to me.

As his health started to decline, Dad began to get angry and frustrated with everything. His anger would be directed toward me, or anything that triggered him. The memories of those moments were stored deep inside of me as guilt and unworthiness.

I remember vividly those painful feelings in my heart and the confusion I felt when Dad became angry. I did not view Dad's anger episodes as a gift until many years later, after he had passed away. The gifts were found within me and had been hidden behind a shadow. Now, as an adult, I acknowledge those gifts with gratitude.

Many years after Dad's passing, I was reminded of the anger he directed toward me, as one of those moments in my childhood re-surfaced. This was surprising to feel. I thought I had forgotten, but deep down it lay buried, returning for me to feel it once more.

I had enrolled in a Transpersonal Art Therapy Counselling diploma course. As students, we were required to visit an accredited Art Therapist. The minimum requirement was one visit per month for twelve months for our personal growth, to learn how sessions felt, and to learn about ourselves before graduating to be a therapist and being let loose with our own clients.

I believed it was to explore our own hidden emotional baggage, to help us set boundaries and be very clear with our clients, and to create awareness of what we carry and what the client is presenting. I found my personal therapy sessions uneasy. Having never been to a counsellor because I did not feel the need to go, I was surprised when I found some skeletons in my psyche closet. I'd always thought of myself as a happy, positive sort of person with no problems that required professional help and had always loved to help other people. This was evident by my work choices, and previously being a registered nurse for many years before starting this course. I had spent many years listening to and supporting patients in my own unique way.

During one of my early sessions with the Art Therapist, we were working on an emotional trigger I had identified that week during class. The therapist guided me into a meditative art session, which bypasses the mind of judgment. I was surprised by the artwork I produced on the big white sheet in front of me. I had drawn childlike figures. One was a very large and intimidating human figure, who appeared to be angry and towering over a little human figure. The little figure was smiling and standing in front of the bigger figure, holding flowers out to the big figure, like a gift.

The therapist asked me, who and what was symbolically represented in my picture.

"I am the small figure holding a bunch of flowers, as a gift offering to the larger figure in the picture."

"Who is the big figure in your picture?"

I surprised myself with how quickly I replied, "Oh, that is my Dad I so loved him and he has passed away now."

A mature adult, I was taken aback by what presented as being triggered at a deeper level. My deep psyche had shown me, graphically, what I had stored in my being at a soul level that needed to be healed.

The therapist continued to ask questions.

"What is this story here in your picture?"

I remembered my father being very upset and angry with me at times. I believed I had made him so angry. I could feel my emotional guilt as I shared the event.

I was a curious child who asked lots of questions, which would make Dad angry. Sometimes he would see my naïve questions as bucking his authority, and that would raise his anger level. On the day I'd drawn about, he became so angry he had his hands around my throat, basically choking me, after pushing me up against the wall. He was out of control with anger.

Mum had to step in, trying to get him to calm down. Wow, that was scary. I only asked him a question so I could understand something. Why did Dad get so mad? I thought at the time. Maybe it was just bad timing? I'm not sure, I was only young.

I felt so guilty and sorry for irritating him, I was not feeling good about myself.

I never felt anger toward him. Why?

Because every time I was in trouble with him, I could still feel his loving heart. I knew somewhere deep inside he did not want to be angry with me, but he did not know how to deal with the frustration and anger he was feeling.

After sharing with the therapist, I was amazed by what I remembered. Until that day I had not thought of this event before. Why did it present on that day? We'd been delving into our childhood memories in my counselling course that week, and although I had felt triggered by one of the other students in my course, I hadn't shown it in class.

When I finished sharing with the therapist, she said, "What a big heart you have, with such compassion and forgiveness. That is such a gift."

I didn't see my unconditional love and compassion as a gift at the time. Didn't everyone have that inside them?

However, when the therapist highlighted this fact to me, I was happy to hear it, and a light went on in my heart and head. It started me thinking that maybe Dad's constant anger was not my fault — he had a problem expressing himself. This was quite a revelation, as I had been blaming myself for irritating him. Then I started to remember many events at school where I had felt sensitive to other students' comments, yet I would always forgive them. I don't remember ever holding a grudge against them, I would just forgive and stay friends.

My insight here:
Behind my shadow I had found a hidden gem and gift not seen before — my capacity to forgive and love unconditionally. The strong guilt emotion was buried so deep in my heart as intense pain, and I did not release it until later. Well-hidden at an unconscious level within me, I'd had no idea how much it affected me by making me feel guilty for both my father's and other peoples' angry outbursts.

After that therapy session my heart felt a little lighter. What else might I find behind the shadows? More gifts! This quote I found recently was helpful to understand my healing.

> *"A child that's being abused by its parents doesn't stop loving its parents; it stops loving itself."*
>
> *Shahida Arabi, Psychologist*

Later that week, I met up with my sister and mother for coffee and shared the details of my therapy session. They both remembered clearly, and with horror, that anger outrage with my father in our home. In fact, they filled me in on all the details I had forgotten and could not recall.

Mum shared that it was a moment that worried her greatly because she had to control my dad's anger and stop him from hurting me. My sister said it was a turning point in her childhood; from that time on, she had vowed not to disagree with my parents or ever share with them her thoughts. She is two years my junior; I think I was around ten or eleven years old at the time.

My memory of the event did not seem to be as dramatic for me as it was for them — or did I just bury it so deep I could not remember the pain, even as my sister and Mum shared their memory of horror on that day?

This new understanding of that incident, and my ability to forgive, did not really change my feelings for my father, as he has always been my hero. However, it did help me see that he had some big anger issues, and when someone is angry it is not my fault.

My self-worth shifted a little at that moment the counsellor told me I had a very big heart and great capacity for compassion and forgiveness. Imagine if all children were given positive messages like that, how much better would they feel about themselves. As a middle-aged adult, it made me feel pretty good about myself. I guess it is never too late to benefit from our healing.

My therapy continued to be a bit of an adventure after that session. I really valued doing the sessions to work with triggers in my life. Learning the techniques to help other people find healing in their hearts was exciting, too. I have been using these art-therapy techniques to bypass the mind in my workshops and find participants gain a great deal from it; I enjoy using this powerful tool myself when I need deeper personal guidance from my soul.

Have you ever found a shadow that was a revelation to you, and that you did not see at the time as a gift?

4

The Family Sponge

My experience of my mother has been very different than my experience with my father.

I've always felt protective of Mum and loved her very much. Unfortunately, I have always struggled to feel her love or support toward me — a major childhood wound that accompanied me into adulthood. It has been a lifelong journey of healing with my mum.

I have felt rejected and unworthy with all the criticisms she shares, so much so my feelings of lack of self-worthiness have been disabling at times. I believe Mum has also struggled from childhood with negativity in her life, and as a sensitive child I took that on. I have always been very good at hiding my hurts behind a very strong, positive exterior shell, but on the inside I am so sensitive and hurting, as I feel other people's emotional pain so keenly.

As I write, I am reminded of the intense pain and sadness I felt as a child, not feeling worthy of or being shown love, making my heart so heavy with grief. Intense pain, suppressed for so many years, rises across my lung area. I had no idea how deeply I had placed this pain into my heart and lungs. It is very uncomfortable to remember how much sadness Mum had around her and how I took it into my heart as a child, blaming myself, trying to get her approval for so many things, so that I might feel worthy of any love she could find for me.

At only nine years old, due to sad circumstances with her parents, Mum was placed in a Catholic children's home in Sydney. Eighteen months later, she was fostered by a family and endured what she described as a very strict and disciplined upbringing. Mum had to care for many other children in the household: four of the children were her siblings, and four others were the foster carers' children, who did not have any restrictions placed on them and were not disciplined.

Mum's childhood duties with her foster family were to do chores, such as the cleaning and washing for the household. There was no time to have fun. Another restriction she experienced was being strictly prohibited from speaking her original family language. Mum's family were Croatian immigrants to Australia, so English was not their first language. They spoke Croatian at home, before she was surrendered to the children's home. If she spoke Croatian, she would be punished by her foster mother. Mum and her siblings had to learn fluent English very quickly from other family members, but even so often felt ostracised by other students during their school days.

Sadly, I can imagine the personal trauma and sadness she has experienced due to separation from her original family at a young age, and then not being allowed to communicate in a familiar language with her siblings. Her family, culture, and language were all taken from her, leaving her with severe limitations in her ability to express herself. I believe this has traumatised her to this day and is why she views her world through fear and negative beliefs, needing to control everything so she doesn't feel extremely anxious.

I believe Mum has suffered an undiagnosed anxiety disorder with post-traumatic stress from a very young age. Many factors in her childhood have occurred for this disorder to manifest. I recall whenever she shared her childhood memories with my sister and myself it was very traumatic and emotional for her. By contrast, now in her eighties, she finds every opportunity to share her childhood story. She repeats it often, to anyone who wants to listen, even outside of our immediate family with people she does not know. It has become who she is — the victim of her story.

Mum does not believe she can change her story to a new version, to find greater happiness by healing her childhood wounds. Her anxiety and fears have affected our family tremendously over the years, like a cloud of darkness. I have struggled to ever feel my mother's love or gain her support. Feelings of rejection, not feeling her love, and my own low self-esteem are wounds I carried in my heart into adulthood.

Now, after healing myself, those wounds have become my gifts and strength for independence.

Do you have a parent, or someone close to you, with mental-health issues? If so, how has that affected your life?

Family members sharing their emotional wounds with me has made me even more sensitive and aware of suffering. I can pick it up very quickly in others. As a young adult, I found it difficult to be in large groups with many friends, because I felt confused by everyone's emotions. I preferred to limit my activities to a smaller group of close friends, but I was always everyone's friend. Being a happy optimist, I wondered why I felt so unhappy and tired after being with some people or groups. Being this sensitive is not such a good quality, unless you understand how to use it to help yourself and others.

I would feel everyone's emotional energy — positive or negative. My heart would feel their pain if they were sad, or I would feel their anxiety and anger, which at times was intense and very uncomfortable for me to feel. I would try to shut it out by not letting them get too close to me, and I would find the friends having fun times, avoiding anyone with intense emotions. I also experimented with trying to fit in with other people's moods to be accepted. This was good if everyone was uplifted and happy, but if they were feeling sad or depressed, I would experience that too; my heart would feel heavy and I would experience tiredness.

In my early twenties, I went to an astrologer for a reading, as I have always been interested in the mystery of life. The astrologer highlighted my sensitive nature as a gift to feel other people's emotions. She may think so, I thought, but I was not so sure, until she explained my full Astrology Natal Chart (life reading from birth). She shared with me, "You are like a chameleon. Being sensitive to everything, your compassionate nature allows you to shape yourself to any situation, because you are an old soul. You have had many earth lives before this one."

This really helped me see myself in a new light. Before that, I thought there was something wrong with me. Feeling aware of all the emotions coming from other people in my teenage years and childhood had been very confusing.

After that, I was able to accept my sensitivity as a gift, and a revelation that I have acknowledged throughout my adult life in a positive way, using it to work with many types of people in the community. Nursing was a good example. I have empathy but learned not to take patients' pain on as mine. With the understanding of my gift, I could still feel the person, but no longer had to carry the suffering of others as my own.

I have found that keeping strong boundaries with compassion is very helpful. Over the years I have noticed that many people in humanitarian work do not have strong boundaries, and I have seen them suffer because of it. It hasn't always come easy. I have had to work at holding boundaries — particularly with my family!

This gift also showed me that when I can feel other people's discomforts and joys, I unconsciously reflect it back to them, like a mirror. Seeing themselves reflected back can help the other person, but many find this confronting. It gets tricky here, because I have had to learn to be very clear of my own boundaries and energy field and what I am experiencing personally, to discern whether I have picked up their emotions or my own. I find this challenging at times, especially if I feel tired or out of balance within myself. If my magnetic energy field is weak, such as when I feel sick or weary, I can take on the pain of others very easily. But life is a learning journey, so I continue to learn personal vibrational healing practices to keep my magnetic field clear and strong.

If I feel someone's negativity and I unconsciously mirror it back to them, this can set up a negative defensive response from the other person if they do not take responsibility for their own emotional shadow or trigger causing them discomfort.

Thanks to Mum showing me I am a sensitive and can pick up energies of others easily, I understand now that I have been a mirror to my parents on many occasions, reflecting their own triggers. Sensitive children can have an innate way of doing this unconsciously to adults. Looking back at my parents' unhealed emotions, I can see that has caused me many problems with them. As a child, I was not aware of this.

I remember my parents saying to me as a young child, "Why do you have such a chip on your shoulder?" I was becoming very defensive and felt not good enough (unworthy). I believe my behaviour reflected my parents' emotional pain and the negativity they hid inside, or perhaps were not even aware of, it was hidden so deep inside of them. I could feel the energy, but I didn't understand how to deal with it.

As a child, so many strong emotions passed through my heart, confusing me. I felt disempowered, wanting to scream how unworthy I felt, that no one wanted to listen to me. My parents would tell me to be quiet and do as I was asked. This often sent me into a rage of frustration, slamming my bedroom door or leaving home saying, "I do not want to go back to that house, they do not love me!"

This pain was expressed at first as intense, passionate energy all through my body. I just wanted them to listen. They would not, so I would feel the emotional anger building through my body, trying to be expressed. I would push it back down, then feel I could not breathe, and would run away to find my calmness and to get my breath. It felt like my breath was stuck in my chest. I felt intense pain and tension I did not know what to do with, so I would just keep trying to suppress it deeper into my body.

I was carrying the pain and suffering of everyone else in my family, something I did not understand as a sensitive child. I thought all the emotional energy around me was mine to hold in my heart. What I did not know as a child was that I was making my own pain-body when I was reacting to those events. I had no idea how to release pain, or how to find the joy in my heart again.

I wanted to leave that crazy house when it hurt too much. As soon as I was back in nature with my family dog, away from the home, the feeling of love returned. That was all I ever wanted — to feel love and joy in my heart. I didn't understand why I had to feel all the emotional tension and pain around me, and no one wanted to talk about it. The elephant in the room – that's what I call it now! We all feel it, but no one wants to talk about it.

When Mum felt triggered, she would use the belt strap on me for a minor misbehaviour she disagreed with. It didn't make sense to me. I'd ask myself why did she need to strap me? Why does she not love me? This is not love!

I reacted by suppressing the pain of my sadness deep into my body. After all, I was only a child, overwhelmed by the intensity of emotions I didn't know what to do with. I did not want to let Mum know though, as I believed she did not care about what I felt in my heart.

I realise now that I was hit because I would not conform to Mum's control. It would trigger her anger and she could not control her own pain within herself, so she shared it with us by using that ugly belt. Thank goodness my father decided to cut the buckle off! The discipline weapon, I called it. When dad was away, Mum could use this belt for any misbehaviour. What misbehaviour? I was a child, all I wanted was to please my parents, to gain their love, and to explore the world.

I remember once borrowing a bicycle with trainer wheels. I was not allowed to have one, so I borrowed my friend's, from down the street. The end wasn't pretty. The training wheels lifted off the ground and I lost control, smashing into our neighbour's car door and making a big hole in the panel. Oops! Lucky my dad was a panel beater and able to do a great job repairing it.

Terrified of what would happen to me, I jumped off the bike and ran inside. I grabbed my Barbie doll and hid behind the living-room door, anxiously waiting, knowing I would be in big trouble for this "misbehaviour." I thought maybe they will not know if I hide here. Of course, they did find me, and I admitted to causing the damage to the car. I have always found it difficult to lie, so I tell the truth, which has caused me more trouble at times.

Heart racing, I was absolutely petrified. What were they going to do to me? It felt like such a big problem for a little child. I was viewed as the bad girl and "disciplined," but the memory was so painful I cannot even recall the details of what they did to me, as tends to happen for me. Being a child, I naively wanted to ride the bicycle, I did not think I want to cause an accident and smash a car door. Is that misbehaviour or just learning?

I believe there are other ways to communicate what is expected, but my parents did not know how because their emotional pain was controlling their minds. Thus, they reacted with physical force toward my sister and myself. I felt we could have had more discussions and talk rather than all the hitting. It did not feel like a safe or happy home for me.

Mum received beltings as a child in her foster family, to discipline and control her, so she believed force was necessary to discipline a child. So cruel, I thought. Children are here on the planet trying to make sense of all this dysfunction in our society. I believe they need love, guidance, and support to find their way into adulthood, not brute force.

I don't remember my father ever hitting us with the belt. He did warn us, "Don't make me get the strap out, I don't want to lose control." I don't think he ever received a belting in his childhood; he came from a very different family life, where love and freedom resided in his home. But he did lose his temper in other ways.

While I shared honestly and transparently with our parents all the feelings in my heart and mind, my younger sister did not. The joy of being a second child, she had the advantage of observing what happened to me when I was being honest. I believe Kim would weigh up the situation and make the conscious choice to make no comment and continue observing.

Maybe I was far too honest with my parents, as I spoke through my heart painful or joyful feelings. I always felt compelled to be transparent, particularly if I felt wronged. Maybe I wanted to gain my power back and to find justice for myself? Looking back as an adult, that transparency caused me a lot more pain. I felt a good deal of frustration and disempowerment in my childhood and teenage years, until I left home and found my way in life independent of my family.

I felt my parents tried to keep me contained in a box with a label. Being a free-spirited and adventurous child caused me great frustration and anger, which I endeavoured to control, another way I was unwittingly building my own pain-body. Living at home I felt controlled, too often unable to honour my own feelings and thoughts. I was not respected by my parents for my thoughts or feelings. This was such a painful experience, I just wanted to leave home all the time, to escape the feeling of being forced to suppress my passion for life. And it gave me great suffering as an adult, to heal and release all my painful emotional reactions to these frustrations.

Have you ever felt your needs were not met as a child, that something was missing for you to feel fully loved by your parents/caregivers?

Sharing my insights from my childhood:
As an adult healing some of my family challenges, I realised my tendency to be a sponge —taking the emotions and pain of my family into my heart with compassion. This meant I had been carrying their pain. I did notice when I was quite young how this affected me. When I spent time with my family I felt heavy and felt the loss of joy in my heart. Later, I would wonder why I felt so tired and drained with no joy.

My intuition would guide me to run away from my home to get the joy feeling back. Time with furry companions and Mother Earth would calm me and feelings of joy and happiness would return.

Why I experienced the feeling of energy draining had always puzzled me. I believe now that as a child I frequently sacrificed myself without being aware of what I was doing. A learning experience here on earth about boundaries, or how to have empathy and compassion without sacrificing myself.

All I wanted in childhood was to be heard, given affection, and told I was wanted, accepted and loved. I believe these are basic needs a child deserves to have fulfilled. My transparency caused me a great deal of frustration from not being heard, and not feeling affection and love from my parents, although I did feel that from a couple of my aunts.

My godmother (Mum's younger sister), has struggled with mental-health issues all her life, I believe from childhood trauma she and Mum endured. She started with post-natal depression, then progressed to bipolar, which took her in and out of hospital where she was misdiagnosed and mistreated when in crisis. Mum has always felt responsible for her younger sister (they are close in age) and has been there for her at those times of crisis.

For as long as I can remember Mum has been seen by the extended family as the matriarch, with an opinion on many subjects. While she means well, wanting to help others, I feel she really has a need to control situations for everyone. I have also noticed when Mum is not in control it causes her much anxiety and stress, likely her PTSD from childhood rising. Dad often tried to console her by saying, "Not to worry." He said that all the time, about everything. I am not sure, but I feel Mum may have also carried some trauma from our ancestors, as her own mother suffered separation from her family.

There was a problem with communication at my home and my role models were struggling with it as well, as they had not been given an instruction book on parenting and communication. Whether it was asked for or not, Mum always gave her opinion, while Dad was very reserved. My role models (parents) were at opposite ends of the spectrum, so to speak: one very opinionated and the other never openly shared his opinion.

I have been an adventurer on many paths, so I explored emotions. I tried Mum's communication approach of being very vocal, to speak up and give my opinion, if I felt it was needed. That got me into a lot of trouble, as Mum would challenge me and we would get into power struggles, causing me pain emotionally and physically.

As a young teenager, I tried Dad's approach of communication by staying silent for as long as I could whenever I was angry and upset. It did not give me any joy. I did get Mum's attention, as

I think she saw it as her challenge to break my silence by trying to get me to talk. I realised later in life that neither approach was in any way helpful to my goal of being heard. My role models did not have the answers for me, so in my adult years I have had to find my own ways to communicate, through learning and exploring with various methods. Life is just so full of learning experiences; this has been one of mine.

Behind these shadows, what I found were my gifts of compassion and forgiveness from experiences with my father. I forgive him for unleashing his anger at me; he did not know how to communicate effectively, with the repressed emotions he suffered.

From Mum, I found my gifts of sensitivity and empathy for others, and my sense of justice to speak up gave me strength of character, while feeling rejected and unsupported encouraged me to find independence in my life. I also learned more about forgiveness: Forgiveness for Mum not having the strength to heal her pain, fears, and grief, as she does not feel safe to be transparent, and for not showing me love. I found love in other people and places, like Mother Earth and nature. Bless my parents for their pain and sufferings.

I share this with compassion for my mother, as she has experienced a very traumatic life, caring for others in her family such as her brothers and sisters in childhood, my father, and her parents in old age. Family dysfunction has been all around her and she has continued to survive with great strength, in the best way she knows.

I believe my mother is an example of how dysfunction leads to the next generation of dysfunction, if we do not heal our own hearts.

Have you found the gifts behind your parents' or caregivers' actions towards you? Do you see any insights in my story for yourself?

5

Generational Trauma

There are no perfect families.

From what I've seen, most families have a degree of dysfunction. Simply because our planet holds so much pain and suffering, we all experience it. The problem is, we keep passing it on to the next generation and think of it as acceptable behaviour!

So how can this be changed? By consciously observing our own triggers of pain and suffering we can start to heal it.

When we experience trauma or pain, we can see it as an experience in our life, or we can keep it as our story that defines who we are, ensuring we never heal it. Holding on to painful memories causes them to be stored deep in your body, in your pain-body, ready to be experienced again and again — every time you are triggered. You probably project your pain onto others too, even though you might be unaware of it. If you are unaware of your triggers, and don't even know they exist, you will continue to suffer from the experience until you release it.

How can you release it?

Becoming conscious of what is triggering you, is the first stage of healing.

Are you aware of your triggers in life? If so, what triggers you? Does someone close to you trigger you to react with strong emotions? If so, would you consider healing it?

As soulful spiritual beings, we are bigger than our human experiences. However, if you see a painful experience as a *human* experience with a lesson to be learned in order to evolve, you can create a new story, one that defines you *without* the suffering.

This will give you more space in your heart for love and joy to enter. Suffering takes a lot of space in the heart, feels heavy, and can be draining on your life force, leaving limited space for joy and love.

I believe I came to this earth as a light being of joy and love, as do all children. Don't believe me? Just look into the eyes of a young baby, watch when they look and smile at you. Have you ever noticed when a baby smiles and laughs how infectious it feels, filling you with joy, too? Even when you do not know why they are laughing you find yourself laughing with them! That is the child's unconditional love and pure heart of light connecting to your soul's light.

As a child, I remember the confusion and discomfort around the emotional and physical pain, anger and suffering I experienced. It appeared to be coming from everywhere in my world. Why was everyone so unkind to others on this beautiful planet? I have always wanted to be here on earth, passionate and enthusiastic to explore my life through my heart. Why was my human experience filled with anger and pain from the family I cared about, and many other sentient beings I observed in my world?

Here is one of my first childhood experiences I remember: I was around four years old and visiting my maternal grandmother in a mental hospital. She was treated very poorly, as a mental-health patient with post-natal depression, which I believe not much was known about in the mid-1940s when she was first admitted. I am not sure it is understood any better today, or do we just have more available drugs to choose from to disconnect us from our heart and emotions? Understanding the side effects of such drugs, as a registered nurse, I have never been convinced they provide a cure or a solution. However, I do know in a crisis (for short-term use) they can be a life saver.

On those visits to see my grandmother (Theresa) I could always feel her love, but we had a barrier with language because she could not speak English, only Croatian. Here is a short version of her story. Theresa arrived in Australia from Croatia on a cruise ship that stopped over in Sydney for two days and was invited to an Australian couple's home for dinner, where she met bachelor Sam (Grandpop), one of the guests of the family. He was also an immigrant, having arrived many years prior from Croatia. Sam had made a life in Australia, purchased land, and was working it as a primary producer of vegetable crops.

Romance was in the air! Sam fell in love instantly and knew he wanted to marry her, but there were many family complications. Theresa's family had already promised her to another man, who she was on her way to meet in New Zealand (an arranged marriage).

The next day, Theresa returned to the cruise liner and continued her journey onto New Zealand to meet her extended family and newly promised husband.

Sam was obsessed, so he kept sending letters to Theresa in New Zealand — until her older brothers and family found out. Apparently, they physically beat her up for disgracing the family and writing letters to another lover. Now it appears so brutal, to learn that women did not have a say in their lives, but at that time family honour overrode all else.

Sam did not stop contacting Theresa — he had an uncle in New Zealand who was happy to deliver the letters secretly. This gave my grandparents an opportunity to meet up in New Zealand. When Sam arrived, they ran away together, got married secretly, and came to Australia, where Sam owned a twenty-acre property on Sydney's Northern Beaches, with a house for them to live in.

Theresa and Sam knew one another from Croatia, where they had lived in the same village on the Dalmatian coast. Theresa was just a young girl when Sam left the village to immigrate to Australia. Sam had not seen Theresa as a potential bride in his younger years, but when he met her again in Sydney she had grown into a beautiful young woman. It was love at first sight.

Sam spoke fluent English, but it wasn't so easy for Theresa, who delivered five children in eight years with no family support in Australia. The responsibility of children and her new farm home to run, all too soon after marrying, meant she had no opportunity to learn a new language or culture. Theresa had been the only girl in her family of brothers, and had many beautiful things bought for her by the family. I am told her life prior to marriage was very comfortable, and she was cared for very well as a young woman without responsibilities.

Our family believed my grandmother struggled to cope with the stress of caring for so many children within such a short time of arriving, as well as dealing with the dramatic life change from her previous life. Delivering her fifth child became a tragic turning point. Theresa had a breakdown (post-natal depression) and was taken to a mental-health hospital, as they were called in those days. Sadly, she never returned to her family or the farm, as she was scheduled category one as an inpatient until she passed away in her sixties.

I wasn't the only one who could not speak with my grandmother. Because Mum's foster family had forbidden her to speak her original family language of Croatian, she could not remember how to speak it by the time she was a teenager. So our visits to grandmother were very limited conversationally. Mum could not even converse with her own mother —how sad is that? I feel for Mum's family, torn apart due to mental illness and with no extended family in Australia, living in an unfamiliar country.

I remember my grandmother being cared for in institutions all my childhood. I found the regular visits fascinating, to see all the strange behaviours of the other inpatients as we walked the corridors and sat with my grandmother in the gardens. This bought on one of my childhood "Alice in Wonderland" moments, when I observed the institution and the patients on my visits. I'm told my grandmother was very quiet and withdrawn until we came to visit. I would see a little smile on her face, and I felt her love toward us. I felt her love in my heart as she held my hand.

I did find a way to communicate later, as a young teenager, by making sure I had jewellery on when I visited. From her reaction, I knew she loved it.

Mum forced me to follow the Catholic religion, so at age twelve I had to take part in a ceremonial event, at which time I would nominate a saint's name as my spiritual name to confirm my Catholic faith. I chose Theresa, my grandmother's name, because I thought she was special and needed some help in her life for all she had endured.

On those regular visits to see her I could sense the pain of the inpatients. It felt as though their minds were being twisted and their hearts were shut down, feeling cold from lack of love. As a young adult, the pain and suffering in the mental hospital was re-enforced to me when I began studying for my nursing career in late 1977 in Sydney. I was surprised and upset by a psychological video we watched, "A Day in the Life of a Mental Health Patient" in the 1940s to the 1960s.

My heart was heavy for days, trying to make sense of all the suffering inflicted on others. The video showed the inpatients of a mental health hospital having a "shower." They were all huddled together naked in a cold, tiled room, while a water hose (similar to a fire hose) was blasted at them to wash them down. I could not believe the video. There was no dignity or respect for those poor souls; they were treated like cattle in a stock yard. I still cannot believe we can treat another person so disrespectfully, without compassion.

No wonder I felt the pain and suffering of the poor inpatients, including my grandmother. I felt they were stripped of their dignity. Thankfully, I believe those institutions have since closed in Australia and we care for people in community homes now. I vaguely remember my grandmother going to a community home in the 1980s, after she had been totally institutionalised for forty plus years! How scary for her; I think it did take her some time to settle into the home.

I remember our family concerned on one occasion, as she disappeared for a day. She got lost going to the shops and everyone was out looking for her. I hoped for her sake she was running away! But I feel her spirit was lost, taken away from her with all the drugs and treatments they gave her over so many years. She had become a shell and dependent on others for her needs. Occasionally, I would see a little light in her eyes. What a traumatic journey she had on this planet. Bless her, hopefully she has now found peace.

Have you, or anyone in your family, been part of the mental-health journey? If so, were you able to help them feel love?
If you have suffered mental-health issues, have you found it challenging to open yourself to receiving love?
Have you ever felt the pain and suffering on this earth?
How does it affect you?

6

Potato Chips and Friday Nights

I remember special days with Dad, when he was home from his weeks away working somewhere in the country. Funny how we remember the simple moments from childhood. Potato chips were a special treat in our home. Dad would bring them out and we'd sit together as a family, enjoying whatever movies he had chosen on the television and eating potato chips. Dad and I had an addiction for potatoes! He loved them, and I loved them even more. I still have an addiction for potato chips; maybe it is in my genes. I felt so happy when he was home because our home was joyful. I loved his sense of fun. Dad was the heart of our home to me.

Sometimes we watched cowboy movies. It was the 1960s, when men liked to watch actors John Wayne, Clint Eastwood, and Paul Newman. I did not really mind as long as I sat with my dad, whom I adored.

Those events remind me of the discomfort I felt in my heart at an early age, of the pain of other species and people. Why were people inflicting pain on one another? Watching an old cowboy movie upset me terribly. It was the horrible deaths I saw on the television screen — cowboys injuring innocent animals, like cows and horses being shot dead before us. I found that very confronting, as I could not watch animals being hurt, maimed, shot, or killed. I had to stop watching the program and turn my head away. I would physically feel the pain, in my heart and chest area.

I didn't understand how my parents could just sit and watch those awful scenes.

"How can they kill those poor animals?" I asked.

Dad's response was, "It's just a movie, don't be silly, Debbie!" But as a child, I would feel in my own heart real pain for the animals being injured. Dad would have quite a job convincing me it wasn't real, that it was just Hollywood pretending.

Still today, I am not convinced it is just a setup when animals are shown as injured for a movie scene. What I feel now is that animals are being exploited for the entertainment industry. They may not die, but they are disciplined to do actions they may not want to.

Dad wasn't around a great deal in my early years, as he found work that took him away from home for weeks at a time. He would return, then off again to another job some place far away. I always looked forward to Dad's homecomings, because he would be happy, and we would have some fun with him on family days together.

Dad took his father role very responsibly as a good provider and protector, keeping us safe. He ensured we were provided for financially and never had to be concerned for our survival needs, not that we were wealthy, as Dad was a working-class man. He always had a job, even though he changed jobs often. Dad was very charismatic and got on with everyone he met, so he was very well-liked, I think because he had such a great sense of humour and sense of fun and he liked his freedom, as Mum found out later. But he would get angry as we grew older, when he stopped working away from home for extended periods.

Mum was happier when Dad came home, until he wanted to socialise with his old mates one night a week at the local hotel. That was when my parents had some big domestic arguments.

I vividly recall feeling the pain around my parents when they argued. It was a big discomfort I felt strongly in my heart. It was so intense because it felt like it happened more often than I would like to remember, so I was unable to forget it. I remember those nights when Dad smelled strongly of alcohol. To this day, I cannot stand the smell of beer, as it brings back memories of my parents' arguments.

Friday nights Dad would have a few beers with his male friends at the local hotel (Mum allowed Dad one night a week with his mates). Other nights of the week he would drink at home with Mum at the dining table, after work and before dinner. This was a ritual in our household. Dad came home from work with two large bottles of beer, then drank both while reading the newspaper and talking to Mum as she prepared the dinner and had one drink with him.

Our home was in the district where my father grew up, so he knew everyone and loved to socialise. I think I also got this from my Dad, as I love to socialise and have had a healthy network of friends all my life, wherever I have lived. I believe Dad had a lot of freedom in his younger years, unlike Mum. I would feel her trying to control Dad at times, and he would simply resist. I am not sure if Mum has ever known or felt freedom in her life, living with all her anxiety issues.

Mum's efforts to control Dad's freedom caused some big arguments. I felt their pain intensely. I don't think my parents wanted to argue, but that is exactly what they did, screaming and slamming doors. I observed those Friday-night arguments triggered by Mum. She'd have dinner cooked and ready for the table, but sometimes Dad would roll in the door a little late. I don't remember him being really late, though — maybe twenty to thirty minutes.

Mum wouldn't give Dad space to think, she would keep pushing him, then he would crack into a ferocious anger, roar and slam the doors.

I don't remember Dad ever being physically abusive to Mum, it was usually words like, "leave me alone, stop nagging me," then silence. I believe Mum would push him with her words to get a reaction — and that is exactly what she got. We all felt it in the house, the roar of the lion. So sad, as I remember my dad was mostly very accommodating of my mother, passive and agreeable, until he had been socialising with his mates and ingested alcohol, then he would try to stand up to her.

I just wanted them to stop arguing and be friends again. My heart felt like it was being torn out of my chest with pain; the two people I loved most in my life were angry and fighting with one another. They did eventually stop, but as a child it seemed like a long time. It may have only been the next day, but Dad would still be very quiet with Mum, responding to questions with a groan. Feeling their tension in my body, I just wanted them to be happy again.

I would go outside and sit in the backyard, where my heart felt soothed just by being with Mother Earth, the birds, the trees, and talking to our family furry companion, Bruno the dog. Mother Earth always gave me so much peace. Here's my personal "Alice In Wonderland" story. I would play the characters aloud, to make sense of my life. As Bruno listened very intently to me, all ears, I would feel him leaning on my shoulder, affectionately loving me.

I spent a lot of time with our dog, talking and sharing my emotions. To this day I have a great rapport with dogs and other animals. They were my trusted friends as a child, listening and being affectionate, hugging me. I felt a lack of affection at home, so my dog filled the gap in my heart, often licking my face with his wet tongue. A game I sometimes played was to howl like a dog, and all the dogs in my street would howl with me. That was a great moment as a child, connecting with all my furry friends and having them respond in a very powerful way.

My parents would tell me to be quiet.

"Debbie, don't do that with the dogs."

Apparently, they were not impressed by my dog communication skills. I loved the feeling of being one of the pack as the sound was pretty awesome, or so I thought. The sound was like when the ambulance drives by and all the dogs howl together. I struggled as a child, not being heard, but my furry friends always listened to me.

They always warmed my heart, they had so much unconditional love for me. I could feel it!

My parents worked as a team when renovating the very old terrace house I grew up in Sydney. Dad had no real trade, but was good at building things and was known to be a perfectionist. He started two businesses on his own, as he didn't really appreciate bosses telling him what to do. The family called him a jack of all trades, master of none.

Dad's occupations varied from fencing and welding, doing electric powerlines in streets, to car restorations and house renovations. Dad didn't want Mum to work, as he saw it as his responsibility to provide for the family. Mum did, however, help with his small business selling renovated cars, as she loved talking to people and selling while Dad preferred to be the artist behind the scenes. He was highly skilled and sought-after by car dealers for his good workmanship.

When Dad's health started to deteriorate during my early teenage years, Mum found part-time work in a department store selling credit cards, then landed a job in a bank, where she was often rewarded with bonuses. Dad still didn't really want her to work, but he had to agree. I believe she enjoyed that job, as it gave her a sense of self-worth and she was acknowledged for her outstanding achievements. It did seem to give her a little more happiness, especially when her bonuses paid for a weekend away.

My parents had experienced vastly different family life before they met. Mum had no freedom, while my Dad had enjoyed all the freedom with no restrictions. Granddad Henry's (Dad's father) forebears were from the United Kingdom. A few generations back, two brothers, both Baptist ministers, came from Somerset in the United Kingdom to set up a ministry for the early white settlers in Australia. Dad's mother, my beautiful grandmother Ivy, arrived in Australia from London at twenty years of age. Ivy had been adopted, so we never knew her original family from Whitehall, in London.

My father roamed freely growing up and did as he pleased with his mates. The freedom Dad expressed in life was the one thing he and I really connected with. I felt he didn't always agree with Mum's restrictions and anxieties, but he would never go against her decisions in front of the children. If we tried to get his opinion, Dad would respond with, "Whatever your mother says is what it is, don't ask me again!" And we did not.

Dad grew up with eight brothers and sisters, plus a cousin, and Great Grandmother Margaret (who bore eighteen children) and lived with Dad's family until she passed in her nineties. Granddad Henry was a fireman and suffered for much of his life before he died from the same disease that took my father.

From the stories he shared, I believe Dad was a bit of a prankster with his mates. He loved playing all sports and the great outdoors, he would go with his friends on long motorcycle journeys and go camping in the bush, shooting rabbits for their meals. I remember Grandmother Ivy as delightfully big-hearted, easy-going and smiling. She was affectionate and gave me the best big hugs. Her heart was open to anyone who came to the family home and food was always on the stove and offered to share. Their house was like a busy beehive, with family coming and going.

Granddad Henry was a very quiet, conservative, private man. In my earliest memories of him he was already quite unwell, in bed and unable to breathe easily. Even so, my memory of him is of joy. He always embraced me and I could feel his love. As I sat upon his bed, aged around four years old, he would listen to my banter and chatter. I felt close to him and my grandmother, as they lived nearby and we saw them often.

In contrast, visits to Mum's foster mother were very solemn and boring. We had to be on our best behaviour, and I always felt Mum was only visiting out of duty. I think she was always grateful for the foster mother taking her and all her siblings into her home and keeping them together, she thought that was a blessing. I did not feel love at that house and did not enjoy those visits. I preferred to visit my grandmother Theresa at the mental hospital, as there was more love there.

Have you ever felt protective of someone whom you love deeply, and then to only feel heartache from them?

I was a shy child with strangers outside of the family network, but I was very protective of Mum and could feel her anxieties rising at times. I didn't know why until later in my adult life.

When I was twelve years old a car came out of nowhere, fast, and did a right-hand turn — slamming into our car as we ascended to the crest of a hill. No shyness that day! I reacted with a fierce, emotional and protective force.

I shook with rage at the scene of that car accident with my mother, little sister and myself. Sitting in the front seat with Mum, I could feel her anxiety, so I immediately jumped out and told off the driver of the other vehicle.

I was trying to protect my mum and sister.

Other times I felt Mum's emotional pain, when my parents had those big arguments. Although I never felt love in her heart toward me, it felt lacking much of the time, for some reason I had this urge to protect her from emotional discomfort.

Mum and I had many disagreements, due to her always controlling me and me resisting. I wanted to break free, to find my own voice and feel empowered. As a young person I found this very frustrating.

Did you ever feel homesick as a child?
If so, what feelings did it present to you?

I never experienced being homesick. I curiously watched many other children away on camps missing their home life, but not me! I thrived away from my family, in the joy of socialising at school and school camps or staying at my aunt's farm with my five cousins in school holidays. I loved to visit my godmother, Aunty May because she showered me with affection and would listen to me. I felt heard, something that did not happen in our home.

One of my cousins came to stay with our family for a short holiday when she was twelve years old. She said it was very noticeable how our home was not so happy, and how Mum favoured my sister and Dad favoured me, when he wasn't angry.

That was a surprise to my sister and me. At that young age we did not really think much of our cousin's comments, but as I have grown older, I believe it was the truth. To this day, my cousin is very perceptive and sees through illusions and shares her truths openly. I think she observed what we thought to be normal as children, we had no other way to gauge it.

I would look for ways to be at my friends' homes to play. If they had lots of brothers and sisters, that would be more of an incentive for me. I loved the laughter, the freedom everyone felt coming and going, and the warm hearts of the family in a messy and busy home.

Those things were not in my home, so I was often at my friends' houses having fun with their families, or we would go off for hours on very long walks for several kilometres, exploring parks, canals, and other suburbs.

I found my home cold, lacking freedom to do as I pleased. All I heard was judgment or criticism, and the chores had to be done before we could even think about the fun side of life — washing windows and mirrors, vacuuming the floors, washing the bathroom, the list seemed endless. I remember I would not even go home for lunch and my parents didn't notice, because they were busy renovating cars and I did not have any reason to go home. I just wanted to be where the fun was and the action of many people of all ages.

One friend was from a family of six children, ranging from older teenagers to younger ones just starting school, so it was a hectic home full of life and laughter. I loved it! Down the road, I also had a friend from a Lebanese family with many children. I would go there after school and their mum would cook us a lovely Lebanese savoury egg dish, like an omelette with many veggies inside. I enjoyed the spices and flavours that were very new for me. Dad did not like anything but simple foods, and that is what Mum cooked, meat and three healthy veggies. Two friends were sisters from France who lived nearby, so we'd play together and they would invite me to their place for lunch, where I tried French food — cheeses and beautiful breads and dips. I was so interested to try new foods and explore new cultures.

7

I Love You

I started travelling at a young age, running away from home often when I was in primary school (pre-teenage years). I saw everything outside of my home as exciting. I just wanted to get away from that feeling in my heart of my family's anxieties, receiving negativity, and feeling the anger and frustration of not being heard. I felt sad that no one loved me or wanted me around. If I tried to spend time with Dad by showing interest in his work on cars he'd say, "Go help your mother in the house." While writing this book, so many shadows have presented that I had forgotten, having pushed them deep into my heart to shut the pain out.

I don't remember ever feeling love or affection. So many judgments and criticisms, and never given credit or inspiring words. So often my heart felt saddened, broken, and empty, so I just kept filling it with adventures and being with other families, and that made me feel happy. Seeing all the wonders of life away from home, I could bury my sadness deep so I could only see what I was experiencing elsewhere. My optimistic nature helped me get through, but the painful feelings I was burying would become the shadows that surfaced so painfully later.

Have you ever felt rejected by your caregiver/parent, because they did not understand you? How did that make you feel?

Often when I ran away from home it was due to battles with Mum, her not understanding me or giving me any affection. Sometimes, when I was tired of walking the streets, I would go to Aunty Jane's house some streets away. She was always interested in what I had to share and I would feel her love toward me at her home, but after our chats she would ring Mum.

"Deb is here at my house."

Mum would come for me, and on the drive home I would feel her frustration with me. I feel she was never able to understand how I viewed the world.

On another occasion in my early twenties I was returning back to Australia after living abroad in Europe for two years. Mum had picked me up from the airport and while driving home I felt she was not interested to know about my journeys abroad. However, Aunty Jane had asked Mum to stop at her place on our way home so I could share with her my experiences and how I felt returning home. I always remember her interest in me as a young person, Aunty Jane gave me such warmth in my heart.

Mum was cranky with me one day and spat out, "It's all right for you, gallivanting all over the world. You cannot keep doing that all your life!" Did she not feel freedom in her life?

I suspect she didn't. Mum has never inspired me to follow my calling to travel.

I am always happiest when travelling, the little gypsy inside calls me to find a home anywhere my heart is happy. Packing a suitcase and going on journeys started for me as a very young child running away, which has been evident all through my life.

A shadow that rose to be highlighted many years later was that I held back on deep friendships, only letting my partners get close to me. Why? Because I didn't want any more painful experiences of feeling rejected and not loved. I have never been short of friends in life, but had only one close friend, as I viewed friendships as for fun times, never sharing those challenging times in life. I guess I did not feel okay to trust anyone else with my heart too closely, it was already broken and fragile.

Finding out timing can make a difference to what we experience on this planet.

I believe my parents were very much in love when they conceived me, but they experienced many changes in their life when I was born, perhaps due to the scarcity of money and changes to their personal freedom. I'm not totally convinced Mum really wanted to be a mother, at least not so early into her marriage of two years. To be fair, she had already been a mother figure for most of her childhood, caring for her brothers and sisters in her foster family home.

I was the first born. Mum told me I interrupted their renovations to the house, and that I was not planned. She shared with strong words, "We were not ready for children until later." Mum never holds back her words, she shared my poorly timed arrival as a matter of fact. I am not sure I would tell my child about this event, even it was true! As a child, this confused me. How did I stop them renovating the house? My unworthiness was already being implanted at quite a young age, by her comments of being less important than the house renovations.

I never heard her say they were happy to have me in their lives. I always seemed to be an irritation, triggering my parents frequently as I often questioned their authority. I wasn't trying to be difficult, I just had an inquisitive mind.

Have you ever been to a psychic/spiritual reader and found out something that gives you a surprising insight?

Only recently, I consulted a psychic/spiritual reader out of curiosity, not expecting him to tell me about my mother. He shared that I was a source of discontent to Mum when I arrived on the earth too early, because my parents had planned children for a later time. Oops! It seems my enthusiasm to be on this planet caused me problems from the moment of my birth. I am not sure how accurate this is regarding the divine timing of events, but it may explain Mum's harsh words in letting me know I'd interrupted their life plans.

Interesting to view this comment as an adult, as one of my lessons in this life has always been to find patience! Should I be surprised by this reading? I hear you — of course I shouldn't! But if the message is correct and I slipped through the net to get to earth early, was that divine timing?

Do you believe we can change these dysfunctional stories to more loving ones, at this time on the planet?

I believe we can turn the stories from dysfunctional families into more positive experiences by being more conscious of our comments and what triggers us. When triggered, maybe someone is showing us a mirror of ourselves.

Do we have the courage and strength to take that emotional discomfort we feel as a mirror, to learn about ourselves and heal our hearts in this life? That would mean being responsible for our own reactions and not blaming others for how we feel.

Still now, when I am being my optimistic self and sharing my hope for the world, it triggers Mum. Quickly she becomes aggravated and upset, then responds with negative words and emotions toward me, and I feel her dismiss me with her comments. Accustomed through childhood to her negativity, which often made me feel unworthy, as an adult I have learned to ignore Mum's negativity. I no longer react defensively as I did as a child. After much self-healing, I know now Who I Am, and no longer need her approval. I believe Mum has done the very best she could with what she had available to her.

This came to light only recently when I was having a café break with my sister and mother. Later on my sister pointed out to me, how Mum reacts negatively towards me when I am my optimistic self and how she immediately responds with negativity and downplays my comments, criticising me and totally disregarding my comments or how I might feel.

My sister highlighted that this reaction toward me was not a normal, healthy response from a mother. When I thought about it, my sister was right. It is not healthy to have all that negativity directed at me. I have a choice to accept the negativity, or not accept it. I have chosen to not take it on personally any longer. I believe it is Mum's own pain and suffering that she is feeling as a trigger, not mine any longer. I have compassion for her anxieties and pain, but I do not need to take them on by emotionally reacting.

As a child, I remember feeling confused in my heart when I triggered Mum with some innocent comment and received a negative response. After healing parts of myself, I know if I emotionally react it becomes my trigger.

I also know how much anxiety and fear Mum carries from her childhood, and how she has never healed it. Thus, it continues to control her, in her unconscious reactions to so many triggers, not just from me, but also from other people and many situations or events in her life. I am sure that is why she feels happiest home alone in her own company. I believe her fears keep her alone and isolated from people and she resists anyone getting too close to her. That sounds familiar to me, after healing that same fear in myself some time ago.

Mum is happiest if we, the family, only visit occasionally and for short periods. And yet, I have noticed she will go to the shops and talk to total strangers, telling them all about her childhood trauma story, then feels very happy she shared it. Is that therapy for her? I am not sure, but if it makes her feel better, then I am happy for her. I wonder what the stranger feels after the long conversation — uplifted, or drained energetically? We all find ways to help us survive and feel better. I sure know all about trying to find happy places, because I explored many ways to feel happier in my younger years.

I felt quite triggered by Mum when I moved interstate with my boyfriend many years ago. I would ring Mum to talk, and ask, "How's life, Mum? Are you going well?" All I would receive on the other end of the phone was a grumpy, "Hello, what are you ringing me for?" That's all I got. Not at all interested in anything but herself and judgment about other people, and never asking if I was okay. Such depressing phone calls! I'd hang up crying, and my boyfriend would say, "Why are you ringing your mother and doing this to yourself? You know what she's like, it's obvious she isn't interested in you and doesn't want to talk to you. Leave her to her own unhappiness."

I never knew if she was unhappy because I moved to the other side of the country, or she was just continuing to not be interested in me, wherever I lived. Not feeling supported continued into my adult years, but I have noticed that if Mum can control a situation, she is interested. Because Mum was so controlling in my childhood, I have learned to be very independent. This has given her no opportunity to control my life as an adult. I often wonder when someone is needing to be in control all the time, what is it they gain from the situation? Is it feeling needed, or a sense of belonging and purpose to help others? Maybe a coping mechanism from not having a sense of power in childhood? Am I controlling too? Yes, in the past when I felt separate from the world and did not trust the divine flow in my life.

For many years I phoned Mum and would end with, "I love you, Mum." Now she is in her eighties, and on occasion I will actually hear her respond in a shaky, hesitant voice, "Yes, I love you." It is wonderful to hear those words from my mother after not hearing them for so many years.

What I have learned is that if we let go of expectations of others, we begin to heal our hearts and the hearts of those connected to us.

Some time back, I became so upset with the unhealthy phone calls with Mum that one day I just knew I needed to spend time with Mother Earth and be in nature. That always soothes my soul and heart. When I did this, I stayed present and felt into my heart to release the expectations I had placed on my emotionally traumatised mother, understanding that she was doing the best she could with the pain she had experienced in her life.

I sat in meditation and communed with Mother Earth, to help me let go of the ties that were binding me to Mum with expectations. In that simple ritual I let her go, to help her be free of my expectations as a mother and to be who she really was — a unique human being having an earthly journey, as we all are.

This was a very emotional healing for me. I immediately felt all the trees around me hug me, energetically. I cried with the sadness of letting go of Mum, but also with joy that I had connected at a deeper level with Mother Earth and she was giving me guidance and nurturing me. I felt so much lighter after my joy returned, and when I spoke to Mum again on the phone I wasn't triggered, as I knew I had found my real mother on earth. Mother Earth has been available to me 24/7. Whenever I need nurturing and love, I feel Mother Earth in so many ways when I spend the time to be in my heart and be present with her energy. That was a blessing and revelation to behold, one of the many gifts, I have received over the years.

Interestingly, I noticed that within a short time after this Mother Earth healing I experienced a small change in Mum's heart towards me.

> *I thought this was a great share, after doing the healing with my mother, because it shows how when our hearts are full of love and expanded, it overflows to others in our life and can help them heal too.*

Dad often said to Mum that she should find a new partner, not to stay alone when he passed. Sometime after Dad's passing, Mum fell in love with a new partner who originally came from her parents' homeland of Croatia. After seeing her in grief for so many months, it was great to see her so happy and in love. I could feel the fullness in her heart. And she was learning about her parents' culture, an opportunity she had missed in her childhood. What a blessing! Even some language came back to her memory. They were together for some years, but sadly did not continue. Sometime later Mum's ex-partner shared with me that they parted ways because she was quite a challenge to be with in a relationship.

My birthday cards from Mum have generally been basic, lacking any feeling content and ending with "best wishes" or "fondest regards, Mum." There was no love, and that's what I came to expect each year. I love to celebrate birthdays, in my childhood my sister and I only ever had one birthday party, which we shared with our cousins. As an adult, I have made sure I celebrate my birthday in passionate ways!

A change occurred within Mum while she was in the relationship with the new partner — she became very happy! For my milestone 50th birthday Mum gave me an extraordinary card, signed by her "love Mum," and her partner, "love Jack." I was a little taken aback when I received it. In fact, it put me into tears of joy and gratitude. The card spelled out some qualities in me I never knew my mother acknowledged. She'd certainly never highlighted these qualities to me ever before! It was the best gift I had ever received, and still makes me very emotional when I read it. Here's what the card said:

"When you were very small, your enthusiasm for life helped me to see the world in a bright, new, wonderful way. You were always eager for the next adventure, fascinated by everything you saw and experienced. You had a kind of magic about you that brightened up even ordinary days. I'm fascinated to see how you handle things and to watch you grow in wisdom and beauty."

Bobby Burrow

You just never know what others are thinking or feeling about you, from their responses towards you and how you impact them. I wanted to frame that card! And privately it has made me cry, realising how damaged Mum has been, too fearful to tell her daughter she loves her and how she viewed me in positive ways, after all these years of verbally giving me so much negativity and criticism. Wow, my heart was full, and I felt it for some days. I try to remember that card now when she is challenging me with her negativity.

Something I feel deeply when I purchase a card for someone is that I wish for the words to inspire the receiver to have a beautiful day, and to make them feel special. That was not my experience from my mother in the past until that card. I feel she does try now, after my positive, loving response to the 50th card. I believe sharing the love does help others heal, too.

When Mum turned eighty, she specified, "I do not want any party or surprises." I honoured her request and arranged a lunch with her extended family, not just the immediate family as she had thought. After the event, Mum did thank me for organising it, she was taken aback by all her extended family; some came from interstate to be there. Mum became very emotional at the lunch as her brother and sisters shared their gratitude for the support Mum had given them in their younger years, as their birth parents were not available. It was wonderful to see Mum so happy for weeks after, I think her family healed her heart a little with all their gratitude and love, which she allowed into her heart.

≈

My insight here:
I believe my parents' unhealed childhood trauma affected how they saw their world. Their perceptions were tainted by fear and anxiety, so their responses tended to be reactionary, judgemental, controlling, and angry, often for what seemed like insignificant reasons. This affected our family in so many ways. I felt controlled as a child, lacked affection and love, and I had unleashed anger sent my way and felt disempowerment that frustrated me. I know Mum was unable to give support, encouragement, or love when I needed it because she never received it herself. With no healing, Mum was plagued by many fears in her life.

Our traumatic experiences in childhood stay with us for life if we do not heal them. If we do not see the triggers that others present to us, we will always be controlled by our old childhood traumas from our subconscious, then as caregivers we react ourselves, instead of responding with awareness to situations. Our wounds from childhood need to be healed, to open our hearts to more love and compassion.

As caregivers, if we do not heal our own wounds we can then pass our unhealed pain on to the next generation, causing more unhappiness and confusion for children as they carry their parents' wounds into their adult life, and the cycle of the wounded child continues. I know this from my own experience, as I have had to heal the wounds I have carried from my family's dysfunction.

We can change this negative pattern if we all look at our triggers and see them as signs of some old hurt we may need to heal within us, hurt that we are often unaware of, as it has been pushed deep into our subconscious pain-body.

If we can just stop and ask ourselves, "Why does this cause me so much anger, for a seemingly unimportant event or reason?" So often, children are the targets for unleashed anger because adults have power over them. Children, spontaneous in their nature, will reflect wounds back to adults like a mirror. Adults may not like what they see reflecting back, but it may help healing, if we are consciously observing. So do we choose to ignore our triggers without healing and keep the cycle of pain going into the next generation of children, as a wound or trauma they take into adulthood, or do we make a choice to heal our own wounds?

It takes a lot of energy to be angry, and a lot less energy to allow forgiveness for what has happened to us. If we allow more space in our hearts, we feel greater love and compassion for ourselves, and then it spreads to others around us.

I also have learned to not take anything people do or say to me personally, for we are all suffering from repressed pain and emotions. Maybe you just happened to be the trigger, whether you know a person or not. If you recognise that we all have pain-bodies and repressed emotions inside of us, you can then recognise that the other person is just a version of you, trying to do the best they can with the resources they have available.

I believe we always need to use compassion to understand the other person, or misunderstanding can cause more pain for you both — and is likely to bring more of your personal triggers to the communication. And that will not go anywhere, just making more pain for you and the other person, or a stalemate situation where no one is happy.

I leave this as a seed to consider, next time you are triggered:

"The wound is the place where the Light enters you."
Rumi

≈

*Have you ever felt the emotional and physical pain from triggering your parent/caregiver but not knowing why?
If so, what did that feel like for you?*

*Have you felt your own triggers from another person?
If so, do you know why that happened? Would you like to heal it?*

*Did you find any insights in my story for yourself?
What were they?*

8

The Caged Lion

Have you noticed we cannot get away from pain and suffering on this planet? It is held energetically in the consciousness of Mother Earth's body, from the past, and every day from the wars and disrespectful actions we commit toward other human beings, Mother Earth, nature and many other species on this earth. I believe much of this pain comes from humans not being conscious of the suffering they are causing themselves, other beings, and Mother Earth. You may know it as karma — when you make your own pain and suffering. I created my own unconscious pain and suffering, until I felt compelled to find a way to release it for my own health and well-being. That was when I found real freedom within my heart, and in this human bodysuit we all wear while on this planet.

On a personal level, we first experience pain as an emotional response to an event, then it becomes a memory stored in the body intelligence as distorted vibrational energy. Triggered, it feels like pain experienced physically or emotionally. You feel the intensity in your body, usually an unconscious action.

Previously, it was thought that the mind held trauma memories. Advancements in body research and new healing technologies provide evidence to suggest that pain trauma is stored as emotional memory and held in the body's intelligence. Yes, the body has its own intelligence, and responds to what the mind is thinking.

I have spent my adult life consciously healing my strong emotional reactions to events that have caused me to feel intense pain in my pain-body. Each time after healing and releasing energy disturbances of trauma in my body, I felt calm and peaceful, centred and balanced. I could not question the concept of trauma memories being held in the body any longer.

Our bodies hold trauma memories as distorted energy, like knots in the body agitating us to react. If we are triggered by a memory or emotion, such as a seemingly small problem we experience, we find ourselves reacting with an emotionally charged response; some may call this overreacting. We may wonder why we had such a strong emotional reaction to a seemly minor event. Maybe it was a trigger that set this up for us to learn about ourselves, our soul wanting us to see it and then heal it.

Have you ever found yourself reacting to a problem, where you felt highly emotionally charged and your reaction could be felt in your body?

Did you wonder why you had such a strong emotional reaction, when on reflection it appeared to be a minor problem?

Charged emotional reactions are held deep in subconscious memory. That is why you often don't know you are being triggered from your trauma and pain-body. Triggers or pain are a way for your body intelligence to send you a message, letting you know you can heal this distorted pain energy in your body right now.

At the time of the trigger, you can observe what happens in your body by being the witness, by not reacting emotionally. Then it will not control your mind, and will release itself. As long as you do not feed it with more emotionally charged reactions it can be released and healed, and the old subconscious habit and judgment memory falls away. When it leaves the body, you will likely feel lighter, calmer, and centred.

This is how I have healed my pain and trauma — by being the observer of my body's reactions when I am triggered. I notice, as my own witness, how that feels in my body. By not giving it more emotional energy from my mind, it has no power and loses the intense energy required to make me agitated.

How can you work with this?

*Consciously observe, be the witness to your reaction
and allow it to arise within you.
Release by witnessing — not reacting again — see it
as your mirror for learning about yourself.*

As a young child, I remember the physical and emotional pain of receiving the strap across my legs. My parents showed us this strap, which was in the top drawer in the kitchen and would be used if we were to misbehave. We were expected to do as we were told without question.

Mum had no hesitation using that strap on my sister and me. I don't remember purposefully misbehaving. In fact, when I think back, I tried to be a good child to get my parents' approval. It confused me that they would get so angry with me when I knew so much about what I needed in my heart. I would vocalise my thoughts when I did not believe in something I was being told, or when I felt to be a voice for animals. Now as I reflect as an adult, I was what you might call a free spirit who could not be tamed and did not conform. I felt my family were always trying to put me in a box with a label, but I could not be confined — I wanted to follow my own intuitive guidance.

I remember so clearly occasions when I did not agree on something with Mum, mostly because she controlled everything and there was no opportunity for discussion. I heard her say so often, "You are the child, you will do what I say in this house!"

One morning before school, Mum used the strap on me for disagreeing on some minor incident that had triggered her. It is etched in my memory, her hitting me angrily with the strap in her reactive state. She gave me angry welt marks striated up the back of my legs, blistered and red.

I believed I must have been naughty, and as a sensitive child did not want anyone to know I had received a belting from my mother. I desperately tried to hide it from my school friends, by pulling my uniform down over my legs. I was about eleven years old and just wanted approval, not to be seen by others as a "naughty girl." I'm not sure I understood why I received the strap on that occasion. I cannot remember anything significant I did to make Mum so angry, but that memory was lasered into my pain-body memory as an emotional and physical trauma, feeling confused about love, because I felt unloved, unworthy, rejected, guilty, and misunderstood.

Have you ever felt the emotional and physical pain from triggering your parents or caregiver without knowing why? If so, what did that feel like for you?

I never felt supported, physical affection, or any remorse from Mum after she strapped us with that belt. I don't remember my father ever using that belt on my sister and I, but he had his triggers and anger issues, sometimes getting verbally short with me, and occasionally losing control and grabbing me physically to release his anger.

I feel now that my parents just did not know how to deal with my independent thinking and free-spirited nature. I could not be put in a box because I followed my heart, there was no label for me. To this day I do not fit into any category of person, as I keep evolving and flowing with life.

I Know Who I Really Am now. I am a free spirit, and that is my blessing.

Have you been punished for questioning adults and felt confused as to why?

Questioning adults sometimes brought unsatisfactory responses. In primary school, I was the kid with the hand up saying, "Pick me, can I help?" I loved school, learning new subjects and socialising with my friends. However, I would get into trouble at religious scripture class as I often chose a class that was not Mum's Roman Catholic religion. I was fascinated by different cultures and religions and didn't understand why I could not learn about them. The teacher would notify my parents, and I'd be told I was very naughty because I took it upon myself to go to other religious classes out of curiosity. Mum would be quite upset with me, another free-spirit moment dampened, wanting to learn more about the world.

My parents always told me they knew best. I always wondered — for whom?

Did you have a compulsory religious practice you had to take part in as a child, with no questions allowed? If so, how did that affect you?

Which brings me to the compulsory church service. Mum, my sister and I "had" to go to the Catholic church service every Sunday. At about eight years old, I questioned Mum about why we were at church. Her answer didn't convince me of anything worthwhile.

"To see God and pray for our sins, we have to," she said.

"Why do we need to come here to see God, when he is here, there and everywhere, and he knows everything?" I asked.

"Just sit and be quiet!" was her response.

This seemed to be the normal response in my early childhood years, just be quiet! It did not answer my questions.

Another Sunday, I asked why my dad never went to church with us.

"As a child, I went twice on Sundays to Church of England sermons, in the morning with grandmother Ivy and evenings with my great grandmother because I was her favourite, so I have been to church enough times for my lifetime," he answered. I listened and thought that was interesting.

I remember those Sundays, walking back from church, descending the hill in our street to a thumping rhythm. All our neighbours could hear it too — Dad's music bellowing out of our little terrace house. Dad often played his music very loud and proud on his super four-speaker quadraphonic stereo system. He loved music, particularly his classical records, and some classic pop music of the time if it had big instrumental pieces, such as one of the *Hot August Night albums by Neil Diamond* — he loved that album!

I would much rather have been at home enjoying music with Dad than at the Sunday church ritual. He always seemed to be having so much more fun at home; he played conductor to his music in the living room and would give me a big smile and happy eyes. His music always made me happy too, as I laughed with him. I believe he went to another place in those moments, which is why it was so loud. I understood that happy feeling, as music transforms me. It was his happy place and has become mine, too.

Although I felt asking Dad questions was a way to connect with him, often when I did, he'd get angry with me. I later discovered that talking music always got a positive response from him. Mum wasn't interested in music that I remember, but she did like to take us to the theatre and enjoyed the music of opera and musical theatre productions. Dad was not a man of many words with us girls most of the time, but Mum made up for that as she talked a lot, filling the gaps for Dad with her chatter.

My insight here:
On many occasions my sister or I accidentally triggered our mother to fly into a rage and punish us with that strap, which she did with a vengeance. I say accidentally because we were children, we had no idea what a trigger was, never mind how to avoid triggering Mum.

My sister always immediately screamed her lungs out, no matter how hard she was hit. Not me! I put my strong silent warrior face on and thought, "You cannot hurt me or break my spirit!" I would hold my breath and make no sound, meaning I was suppressing all my emotional and physical pain, pushing all that frustration and anger deep down into my body.

I remember Mum hitting me harder and for longer than my sister, and I thought it strange. Mum would stop strapping my sister first, then eventually me, maybe when I finally cried and possibly said a few words to her in anger? I believe she worried about what the neighbours might think on hearing all the screaming and commotion, as my sister's screams were deafening, I can still hear them today.

I received more punishment because I made no noise outwardly for such a long time, not wanting to bring attention to our home. All that suppressed anger and pain would be released later in my life. If only I'd known then that I was creating my own future suffering.

Another time, I upset Dad and he hit the table so hard my porridge went all over my school uniform. I had to go and get changed, and it was clear to me that he had become really mad that day. He often said, "Don't you make me angry, because I do not want to hurt you." I believed him when he said that.

Even though all that anger was passed on to me, I could always feel my father's love and I always knew he did not want to hurt me. I felt his remorse when he'd been angry with me; in those moments I knew his life was out of control with all his frustrations. I now understand that both my parents were being triggered by their own pain and suffering in their pain-body.

I never felt Mum's heart beaming toward me, but always felt I wanted to protect her from any heartbreak. If she was upset, I could feel the tension strongly in my own heart and sometimes felt I wanted to cry for her.

I felt disempowered and not heard by my parents.
Did you ever have that feeling of disempowerment as a child?
How so, did it affect you?

I always felt I knew the answers within me, but no one would believe me or wanted to hear me as a child, which made me feel frustrated and emotionally charged inside my body.

Writing this book, as my heart started to heal it felt like I had a caged lion inside my heart who wanted to be released from my chest. It sure felt like a huge force being released! It caused me so much discomfort, as I had to experience all the tension in my body again to let it go.

I was not expecting so much healing after previous years of healing and releasing. Wow. Raising my vibration by releasing stuck energy has been such a challenge for me.

Feeling this pain right now, I feel tension crushing in on my chest. It is so intense I start to feel like I cannot breathe properly. I don't want to feel it, but it has returned, so I consciously allow it to be released as I stay present and witness. This has made me so aware of how we make our own pain and suffering. Now I know why I felt like I had a breathing disorder when I was having challenging times in childhood — it was me trying to deal with each painful experience the best way a child could, by pushing it down, not wanting to feel it anymore. I was taken to the doctor at one point to have tests, as I felt I could not breathe, felt I was suffocating. My test results were negative, clearly showing how our emotions can affect our physical body.

Until I started to release these shadows and my reactions from childhood events later in adulthood, I had no idea how much was held deep down in my heart and chest area or how it was triggering me. It was as if my parents were passing it on to me, the next generation. I have learned how I created my own pain each time I reacted when emotionally charged, and that it is imperative not to react outwardly or suppress my emotions in challenging times.

My learning has been to be in a neutral mind space. That is where you go when you meditate, the most powerful tool to learn as a human being. Imagine how powerful meditation could be for our children, if they learned to meditate at a very young age in order to deal with their emotions with awareness, learning not to create more pain and suffering for themselves. They would experience the neutral-mind awareness of meditation practice, which promotes peaceful mind and calm body, and would grow to be adults and parents with full awareness, not passing their pain and suffering on to the next generation.

We could have an evolved human race on this earth, walking in joy and peace. I have done meditation stories with young children and found them so open to this type of practice. They loved doing it, and I found it helped them feel empowered to find answers for themselves.

9

Culture and Curiosity

Have you ever had a knowing of what is right for you inside your heart, but felt no one was listening? How did that make you feel?

When I was ready for high school, aged thirteen, Mum said I was to go to a Catholic Girls' College, a private high school in Australia— no discussion. I didn't want any more religion and indoctrination from the church being forced onto me. I already had to go to church every Sunday; that was enough as far as I was concerned. I felt the church was hypocritical, as I did not hear love in the teachings, rather they shared fear stories with the congregation. Anyhow, I thought my parents never really gave me any worthwhile reasons to go to church.

You may have already guessed, but I was not going to that Catholic college. I pleaded with my mother, but she never listened. I lived closer to a girls'-only public high school, where my primary school friends would be attending. I decided to leave home and packed my bag. No surprises there! Eventually Mum came to her senses and agreed with me, as she knew I was not going to be happy attending the religious school. I think Dad had a talk with her, as he was not that excited about the church.

I experienced many cultures in my public high school. Due to the demographic of working class and multicultural families, I felt the struggles many families experienced with limited resources. As it was a small high school, we all knew one another and I enjoyed being friends with everyone, whatever their culture. My friends were very compassionate girls from many parts of the world. Fellow students voted me to be a School Prefect (students who are positive role models and provide leadership to the school), which surprised me at the time. But I do remember how I embraced the role responsibly and honourably.

The school had a wonderful and eccentric art teacher who was well-travelled and shared her stories with us. I found her travel tales mesmerising, and she inspired me to travel even more than I had already planned to do, if that was possible. One of the stories was of her female friend who was kidnapped in Turkey to be taken to an Arabic country to live with a Sheikh. Fortunately, she got away before she was transported to that country and was uninjured. I believe that story saved my life later, when I travelled to Europe backpacking. I share this to show that maybe I knew at a soul level that this was the right school for me for my life path, which will become clearer in a later chapter.

In a science class the teacher asked us to raise our hands if we spoke another language at home. In a class of thirty girls, only about four of us didn't raise our hands. I loved that my school was so interesting culturally, as this fed me every day with information about other places and cultures to go see and learn about. I spent time with students from other nations at lunch, and they shared their food and stories about their cultures and what women were expected to do. I was surprised and fascinated by what they shared. I knew I was going to be a traveller, and they were feeding my passion to follow my heart.

When I left the Girls" high school to study at Secretarial College for twelve months, I met Sarah, who quickly became my best friend. Sarah had attended the Catholic Girls' College I had refused to go too at thirteen years old. If I had attended the Catholic College would we have met many years earlier? Is that destiny, that we would eventually meet one another at a different college. When we completed our Secretarial College course, Sarah married and I was invited to become the godmother of her first-born, a beautiful daughter, Anya. I felt ecstatic she would offer me that very special role, a blessing to behold.

10

Dogs and Me

My distraction as a child, not knowing about meditation, was going outside to be with Mother Earth to breathe in all the beauty she offers, and spending time talking with our family dog, where I found great comfort. He was a great listener and gave me loving cuddles, making me feel very happy and loved.

I had a great affinity with all the dogs we ever had in our home, plus any strays Dad may have brought home. I was the one who spent the most time with our family companions, playing and talking with them; they were my besties. When I meet dogs, they often come to me and let me shower them in love, and sometimes they will lay down, taking it all in, unable to resist the love and attention.

I recall my father's love of dogs, like me. One of the early jobs Dad loved was to work outdoors, often around commercial sites he was fencing. Those jobs would take him away from home, sometimes for weeks at a time. He'd come back with stories, and sometimes a little gift for my sister and me. One gift was a beautiful opal bracelet, I loved that present.

One day, he came back with a little puppy with frost-bitten feet he'd found lost on the side of the road. He was driving home on a winter's icy road and spotted a little black and brown pup looking lost and hungry, so he picked him up. Unable to find the owners, Dad fed the dog and bought him home. I was so happy! Another dog for me to play with! He was maybe six months old and so cute and friendly. I don't think we had a dog at the time, so we kept him for a short time, until Dad decided the pup needed a bigger yard than we could offer. He was a little kelpie/crossbreed working dog and was very active, so we took him to live at Grandpop's farm where he'd be free to roam.

When we next visited Grandpop I did not see the kelpie dog anywhere; normally he would greet us.

"Where is he?" I asked.

"He was bitten by a brown snake, he died."

Oh no! I felt so sad, poor little dog — we'd sent him to his death. Grandpop knew that snake very well, they just kept a wide berth of one another all the years Grandpop was living and working on that farm. They had no incidents, but the little dog did not know about this respect for the deadly brown snake, he must have tried to play with the snake, as pups sometimes do. Grandpop lost a few dogs to the snakes on his property. He also had cats, but I think they were a little wiser about the snakes, so they survived living on the property for many years and had many kittens. However, there was room for everyone, so Grandpop just left them to be free and fed them when they arrived at the door, or we did when we visited. I loved visiting Grandpop on the farm, there was twenty acres to roam freely, exploring the natural bush areas which backed onto a national park, and sometimes after our visit Mum would take us to the nearby beach.

I feel the pain of other species in my body and heart.
Have you ever felt the pain of other species in your body?

I remember our family dog, a very proud black and brown coloured Dachshund dog that Dad had named Bruno. You know the type, little dog with big bark, fearless, but also a patient personality with children. I was eleven years old the day I took Bruno for a walk and we passed a house where a Dalmatian dog lived. The gate was open to the yard, but we did not see the dog watching us as we passed by.

Suddenly, he charged out of the yard and attacked Bruno. I couldn't do a thing. I tried to pull them apart, but as a small girl I had no strength. I probably made the situation worse, trying to help by pulling the collar to separate the two dogs. I could see my little Bruno was losing, and the bigger dog was standing over him, biting at his neck.

When they eventually separated, I could see that Bruno's neck was badly torn open, like a knife had been used. The insides of his neck were exposed and bleeding.

I was emotionally devastated, angry, and upset. Even though it was a major road in the suburb, I could not see or find any adults in the street, no one heard or saw the attack. I gathered all my emotional strength to pick up my dog. I carried Bruno in my arms, bleeding, all the way home, whilst I cried and screamed at the pain he was in.

I felt his pain in my body too, it was just too much pain for a child to see and deal with. Finally, I arrived home. Mum patched Bruno up and we took him to the university vet clinic. He eventually recovered, thank goodness. I have never forgotten that traumatic day with my beloved dog.

Another time, we were at a relative's place for an extended family social gathering. I was outside with my cousins and heard a great commotion and screaming in the neighbour's yard. The children all looked over the fence to see what was happening. I wished I hadn't, because what I observed was hideous. I could feel all the fear that chicken was experiencing in my heart, because the neighbour had chopped her head off and the poor chicken was running around the yard headless. That was so painful for my heart to feel. I felt the chicken's confusion and pain. My cousins thought it was funny. I thought how could they be so mean?

No wonder I have been vegetarian most of my life and am now vegan. I just cannot see animals hurt or mistreated in any way; my heart feels as if it is being wrenched out of my chest because I feel their pain. That was the end of my idea of helping animals as a vet nurse when I left school. I just couldn't do it because I would feel all their pain — so I needed to rethink that career!

> *Experiencing the pain of grief in my heart as a child....*
> *Did you experience the death of your furry companion in childhood? If so, what did that feel like for you?*

At sixteen years old I was walking home from school when a tiny little white, black and brown puppy, a miniature Fox Terrier, ran along the main road. It was a busy road, a major artery in Sydney. The little pup came over to me and I picked her up. I noticed no collar and she was very young, three months old maybe. Very small, she fit into the palm of my hand. She looked confused and nervous, so I took her home to keep her safe, planning of course to keep her as my furry companion.

My parents had other ideas.

"No, you cannot keep her!"

I was confused. Why not? We had no dog at the time, as Bruno had died due to an inoperable back injury he'd sustained.

She was so small, she wouldn't eat much or be any trouble. "I will look after her," I told my parents. They were insistent I had to take the pup to the pet shop in the next suburb and there was to be no further discussion. I took her to the pet shop with great sadness and reluctance. My heart was broken. Every day after school I took the long way home to visit the pet shop and check on her and talk with her. After one week no one had purchased her, so I asked my parents, "If no one buys her soon, can I have her back, as she has no family?"

The reply I received was, "No, we told you our answer."

Finally, after a couple weeks of pestering, my parents gave in and agreed to let me take the puppy home. I named her Mandy. My friend Lorraine from across the road was given a gift from her grandparents, a little puppy cattle dog, and our pups were around the same age. Excited, we decided to train our little dogs together each day. We would hit our little dogs to get them to do what we wanted, not hard, but a hit on the bottom to follow our commands such as sitting, lying, and standing still.

After a while, I realised I was doing what I had been shown by my parents — I was hitting to discipline someone I loved! This was not a loving way to get another being to understand my language command. I don't like being hit, why would my little Mandy? She was trying to do as I wanted. I started to give more love and encouragement to her, something I never remember receiving as a child when I needed it. I loved little Mandy so much, I would go everywhere with her. She was always by my side and everyone knew her as my best mate. When I got my driver's licence, she was my special passenger.

Two years on, I was camping with my boyfriend Jason, who also loved Mandy, and he had taken her to the shops to get milk and a newspaper before I rose. When Jason returned to our campsite, I asked, "Where is Mandy?"

"She's in the car. I am so, so, so, sorry. She ran on the road and under a car at the shops and died instantly."

I found her in a cardboard box in the car — dead! I was totally shocked, devastated. This was my very best friend in all the world, we did everything together, now she'd been taken away from me.

Mandy was my first experience of feeling grief. We buried her in the bush overlooking the ocean, as she loved our camping trips at our favourite campsite near the ocean. I had to wait a day to bury her because I could not believe she had died. This haunted me for many months, which caused me to have anorexia from grieving her, my very own beautiful furry friend. I just could not eat anything; I refused to eat.

Heartbroken, I was in a dark place, not wanting to be on the earth without her. Mandy, my best friend, had vanished from my life. I would not see or feel her again. My heart felt wrenched with pain from the grief, I did not want to talk to anyone or do anything, my heart had lost its joy and love had slipped away.

It was an intense experience of death, grief, and loss. I kept having nightmares that she was still alive, that we had buried her alive. This caused me to withdraw from everything in my life, mostly not eating, not interested in going anywhere. I would go to the park and think about her and the times we had together. My heart felt like it was bleeding love. Mandy had died, let her go, she has gone, my family would say. They did not understand the love I had for Mandy. Such a sad time in my life, I was stricken with grief for many months.

I did get a message from Mandy, during a meditation many years later, to say she was always around me and still is, that is why I could feel her near me and why I was confused about her being alive. Mandy had come to teach me about grief and loss at an early age. To hear and feel her around me again brought me to tears. What a blessing that message was. Bless her.

My boyfriend felt so guilty with all my grief and suffering that some months later he brought me a beautiful white Labrador pup. My parents didn't approve, but they had trouble saying no, as I was so depressed. He was a very cute puppy, white and fluffy like a teddy bear; he was huggable and adorable. I did still miss Mandy, as no dog will or has replaced her. Mandy will always be with me in my heart, we had such a strong bond from the first day we found one another on that busy road. However, this little pup did help me release my grief for Mandy.

I was eventually distracted by the new pup, who I named Sabastian, my new furry friend. I had a very different relationship with Sabastian as I did not choose him, he was my boyfriend's gift to me. Sabastian instinctively took on the role of my protector. If I was walking at night and Sabastian did not like a male passing me, he would bark at the person if they came too close, telling them to keep away. His protective side was a surprise, I hadn't had a dog like him before.

I decided to take Sabastian to a dog-training obedience school, and that was revolutionary for me, as dogs were never hit — we used our voices to command our requests and to encourage behaviours, as I had done with Mandy. Some trainers used treats; I never did with Sabastian as he was so enthusiastic to do whatever I asked of him. If he was having loads of fun with me and getting lots of love, he would do anything for me. He knew all the commands by sign language, without me speaking. He stood out as the smartest dog in the training class and I was the best student as I learned to communicate with Sabastian, who learned so quickly.

My father was fascinated to see Sabastian working with me, because he knew all my silent commands, using hand signals and lots of love and encouragement. Sabastian and I had many fun times together, he was by my side wherever I roamed, and we were always going somewhere such as the beach or a park to explore our favourite place. He would travel beside me with his beautiful big white head hanging out of the car. He loved that feeling of the wind on his face. When we got within a few streets of the beach he'd start talking and barking, and look across at me like, "Wow, we are going to the beach?"

Two years on grief struck again. I had been working nightshift as a nurse, and Dad noticed Sabastian had not been out on his daily walk with me, so he let him out the gate. Down the street Sabastian ran, and straight out across the road in front of a motorbike. The bike rider was okay, but Sabastian died instantly. I couldn't believe it.

I knew how much my dad loved Sabastian, and just knew he was feeling guilty and so awful in his heart for being part of Sabastian's fatal accident, but I never blamed him. I remember how proud Dad was when he watched Sabastian and me training. He admired my training skills and saw what a special gift it was to have Sabastian, so attentive to me without any treats, just my silent language signs and lots of love and praise.

Dad even complimented me on my trainings, once. Now that was quite a moment in time — for me to get praise from my father! Dad didn't give compliments, so I felt very special to receive any feedback, and because you never knew what Dad thought, most of the time anyway. It seems my dog-training activities opened him up to tell me. I remember hearing Dad talking to his mates one day about how his daughter could communicate with her dog by using sign language. This gave me a rare moment of feeling I had gained Dad's approval.

≈

My insight here:

My training with Sabastian was an opportunity to help my family see that you do not need to use force to have another person or species understand your language or your wishes.

The strangest thing is that both times my dogs were killed on the road they were not with me, and neither of them had ever run out on the road with me. The grief from Sabastian's death upset me very deeply, but I didn't become anorexic this time, even though it took some time to release him. It was a very different grief experience.

I kept thinking it had happened for some reason — maybe he was taken from me because we were never meant to be together any longer than that, our time had ended, as if it was written somewhere in the big blue sky. I knew I had to move on to a new journey, and I had been planning my overseas dream trip. Now that I had no furry bestie to come home to, I decided not to purchase a return ticket home to Australia. This would be a new journey of freedom. That was my optimistic thought as I tried to see the situation in a brighter light, as an opening to move on.

My nursing studies were also coming to an end, as my final registration board exams were scheduled for the coming weeks. That distracted me and helped me to stop thinking about Sabastian every minute, how I was missing him and the fun times we had together. I loved Sabastian so much, but I did believe it was time to let him go much sooner than I had with Mandy. In saying that, I am still not sure if that was because Mandy and I chose one another and Sabastian was chosen for me by my boyfriend, so my connection was different with Sabastian.

I always thought of Sabastian as a bit like me in personality: friendly, open-hearted, enthusiastic, loved life and his freedom, looking for fun and adventure all the time, and of course very affectionate. He was my fun friend and protector, I always felt so safe with him.

Sabastian did get me into some problem spots with his questionable manners. When he was twelve months old, I was standing at traffic lights with him on the lead when he lifted his leg to wee on the trousers of the man beside me. I could clearly see a wet line on his trousers! I was a teenager, and terrified of what the man might do. Fortunately, the trousers were loose, so he hadn't noticed they were wet. When the light changed, Sabastian and I charged across the road and made a run for it. We got away with it, and I was saved from a dry-cleaning bill and any anger response that could have occurred.

Another time Sabastian and I were at the beach — he loved to ride the waves into shore whilst I was on my surf mat. One day Sabastian took the opportunity to ride the wave into the shoreline on the back of a male bodysurfer. I watched the man's reaction when he landed on the shore, and his angry face at my Sabastian, he was looking for the owner. As I watched him from the deep blue sea, I decided to stay out in the waves and not go back to shore on the next wave, so Sabastian would not come to me. I probably would have been in trouble for having my dog roaming freely on the beach without a lead.

Life can be crazy and scary at times when you have an adventurous furry friend like Sabastian. He was a funny dog, got me into all sorts of predicaments. I so missed him and all our crazy adventures we had together.

I have always felt I did not have a voice as a child and felt sensitive to the pain of others suffering around me. In particular I have felt a strong heart connection to animals, as they also do not have a voice to be heard.

Do you have any memories of animals suffering, because they did not have a voice to be heard? How did that feel in your heart?

11

Heart Calling

If I had learnt meditation skills, and the suffering of others was not shared with me, I can only imagine how different my childhood could have been as a sensitive child.

Have you taken on emotional and physical pain from your family? If so, have you found any insights from my story for yourself?

I have taken the emotional and physical pain from my family, however there has been a positive outcome after many years of consciously evolving and healing my heart. What I have found now, as a more conscious human being, is that these shadows have helped me find strength of character and the independence to survive by finding ways to cope and learning to love myself. We cannot rely on others to give us self-love, it comes from within us. For me, it comes when I heal the shadows of unworthiness. When my heart healed and gave me space for more love and compassion for myself, then it went out to other beings and Mother Earth.

How did you survive your childhood?
Did you need to find ways to cope and survive dysfunction in your family?

How did I survive the dysfunction of my childhood, of my home life?

Being an eternal optimist, my way of coping was to believe my own stories. I had a happy fantasy life as Alice in Wonderland — my favourite fairy tale. All the characters were in my life; the wise, the crazy, the wicked, and all the animals and insects talked. I could relate to them all in my own little childhood world, in my family, and out in the backyard when I communed with all of nature in my happy place. I even dressed like Alice for our school fantasy dress-up day. I would run away from painful feelings at home to the lands outside in nature, where I felt loved with my furry companions.

The truth is, I felt it was cold at home, lacking love, respect, freedom and empowerment, and I did not have a voice. I coped by leaving home, to find fun places in nature or in friends' places, until I was old enough to leave home permanently and go on bigger journeys to find the fun, joy, and love that awaited me. I never felt homesick. I believed there was so much excitement away from my home, where I found more love, support, acceptance, and inspiration.

This was my fairy tale for many years, and I believed it. I told everyone how wonderful my childhood was, with memories only of the good times. But underneath, I was unaware of the pain I had stored in my heart and body, with triggers presenting that I did not understand and could not identify.

Believing my make-believe story of a happy home well into adulthood meant I kept the pain pushed deep into the bottom of my heart, and shut the doors on all the suffering stored in my body. I never complained about my childhood, I accepted that is how it was for everyone. I believed my physical needs were met in childhood, that is, I was kept safe and healthy with good wholesome foods and we had occasional holidays together, even though we did not have a great deal of money. But emotionally I felt let down, and this caused me to carry sadness deep in my heart.

I had no idea my painful emotions were separating me from close relationships, due to my fear of being let down. If your family does not provide the emotional support you need, who else can you trust? It was so deeply locked in I could not see these shadows until I was older and started healing them. I have become more conscious over time, and found parts of my heart again after releasing the pains. Now, when old pain arises, I acknowledge, accept, and reflect on how it has shaped my life, relationships, and how I coped with those feelings whilst being unaware of the impact it actually had on me.

In the past, I often became angry if I felt triggered. When I started to release my shadows and accept them, my heart began to expand, opening to new levels of love. My inner wounded child began to heal, and old feelings of connection to the world, and my sensitivity, returned with the expanded heart of love for everything. Gratitude started to become a strong aspect in my life.

This gratitude and acceptance of my shadows has unveiled so many blessings. As the real love surfaces I keep seeing with new eyes and feelings of excitement. I have the curiosity to explore like a child with naïve innocent eyes, no longer judging myself. As my wounded heart began to heal, everything in nature started to talk to me through my rewired heart and soul connections, as they had done in my childhood.

A new level of consciousness unfolds within me and continues to grow deeper as time passes. I feel so expanded, and notice how I start to affect many who are connected to me, giving them space to feel their own hearts and feel more love. It is a green light for others to heal. Feeling safe in the warm heart that is surrounding them, they then feel safe to let go of their own shadows and heal their hearts too.

Only unconditional love has the power to do this for other beings – that is what I have experienced and felt in my own heart.

There are so many layers to our evolution of the heart and soul. The more expansion, the more we find to release at deeper levels, taking us to new levels of consciousness. More magic presents to me each time I let go and my consciousness is raised. I am aware of the painful shadows locked deep in my psyche and heart that have affected my life, and I feel my soul is rising above the anger and fears to find greater love, as the immortal soul I am – and we all are. I feel I am returning to my childhood innocence, from whence I once came.

I believe we are blessed on earth at this unique time to have the opportunity to evolve many lifetimes in this one life. Mother Earth is evolving on a grand scale, and we have so many old souls who have incarnated here on earth before and have been through evolutions with the planet. Our guides and ancestors, they have great wisdom to share and help us all when we call on them. The healing and consciousness raising would normally take many hundreds of incarnations to achieve what we have available to us here in this life right now, as the planet is expanding to a new level of conscious awareness of peace, joy, and love. Some of us will be ascending as masters, if we can heal our hearts in this lifetime and step up to raise our consciousness.

> *Our souls are immortal, and earth is a school to raise our consciousness. We come to earth to wear our human suits, to experience emotions and love.*

It is a privilege to be present, to be part of these great times of evolution on this planet, as many souls are waiting to come to earth to be born, to take the opportunity to accelerate their growth and evolution. Not everyone can come to earth who is waiting to incarnate, so if you are here, feel blessed you have this opportunity to raise your consciousness in order to evolve and raise your personal vibrational frequency to find peace, joy, and greater love and light in your life. As scientists have acknowledged, the universe is ever expanding and so is our planet who births us, Mother Earth.

> *As a small child, did you ever feel your connection with Mother Earth as wonderment and curiosity to explore the outdoors? If so, can you remember those feelings?*

As a very small child, I felt the suffering on this planet and it caused me to look for ways to not feel the pain. As I have shared, I loved to be outside and explore in nature with my dog and all my friends in the garden. We would talk, as I could hear the sounds, songs, and whispers of the natural world as I sat on the grass watching them all go about their daily business. To this day, when I hear birds singing in the trees my heart starts to sing, too.

As I grew older it became necessary for me to be outside, as I felt accepted and heard by nature and my dog. This was a tremendous relief from the pain of my family life and the restrictions imposed on me, of not having a voice or being heard for my own wisdom and inner guidance. My heart felt so open when I was outside, the pain seemed to melt away watching and communing with the natural world.

I remember one day, in my early years, I was so fascinated by the insect world that I was sitting on the grass and a bee stung me. I cried, then Mum took me out to the front yard to play in the clover and within half an hour I was stung again. Apparently, I was trying to pick bees up to carry them with me. Funny how my name, spelled as Debra, means Bee (always busy); that has certainly been my experience in this life. And bees have stung me many times, particularly in childhood. I'm blessed I do not have any allergy or fear of them. I still love bees, as I find them so fascinating, watching their activities on the flowers, collecting for their community hive.

I remember so many times during those power struggles with my mother, when my heart could not take any more pain. I'd pack my little suitcase, take my dog, and leave home, walking the streets for hours. It always felt more exciting away from those old, cold feelings at home. I tapped into new experiences, wanting to find new and exciting things to explore. My travels started at a young age!

One night I watched my uncle's world-travel slideshow with our extended family, after he had returned from travelling the world over several years. I was about twelve years old and made a conscious decision to be on that journey when I grew up, that nothing would stop me. I was going to see the world and all those amazing places for myself.

Being a teenager can be confusing!
Do you remember your life as a teenager?
How did it feel for you in those years?

In my teenage years I spent my time with the beautiful young Jason, who I believe was an angel in my life, a kindred spirit. Jason *really* listened to me, and we shared stories on the suffering we saw on this planet that we both felt in our very young and naïve hearts. In our early teenage years we loved to go on travel journeys together, so we would go on bush walks and train rides. As we became old enough to get our motor-vehicle licences, we would travel far afield to national parks and coastal areas many hours from our homes, just because it was fun to explore.

Jason, my first boyfriend, adored me when he finally got to meet me after watching me for many weeks. He planned an introduction through his sister, who knew my sister. I had not even noticed him in our street, but he had been watching me from his bedroom window, he told me later. Bless him. That beautiful soul Jason became my lifelong friend. Even when we travelled different paths he was always there, protecting me or checking on me. We always had a special bond, seeing the world through our sensitive eyes, wondering why everyone was so angry and not happy here on planet earth.

I think of him as my shining-light friend, because we came to planet earth together in the same year, 1958, and we had many deep conversations and experiences together in our teens. We would sit in his bedroom with the purple light going around while we contemplated the world around us, listening to music from that era: Pink Floyd, Deep Purple, Bob Dylan, David Bowie, Lou Reed. We shared our disappointments with the planet and how people treated Mother Earth and one another.

We were on the hippie side of life, our philosophy, "Make Love, Not War" was what we truly believed. We had older friends in their twenties who were well ingrained into the hippie lifestyle and we admired them. Jason was so sensitive; he would write me songs and poems themed on romance or nature. I remember that after we moved out of home, on the first night in our new flat he sat on the end of our bed and sang me a song before going to sleep. I felt the romance and beauty he shared.

That was who he was, a generous, openhearted soul. He was always so romantic, giving me flowers, cards, and beautiful poetry. This inspired me and gave me hope that I was not totally alone, that someone else could see and feel all the suffering on this earth, too. We had a very special bond as each other's first love. He taught me to communicate with the opposite sex, as I had always been very shy to have conversations with boys. I did attend an all-girls' high school — that probably didn't help me — and Dad was my first male role model and he didn't communicate a great deal with me. We would not know what he was thinking unless we upset him.

My teenage memory with Jason was a beautiful, heart-warming time in my life.

In our mature adult years, we would talk on the phone a few times a year. Jason would call me to catch up on news and check in that I was okay. Sadly Jason died in a car accident, at age fifty-two. I was so shocked! How could life be so cruel and unpredictable? We never know when death is ready to take us on our next journey, away from planet earth.

On the night before Jason's fatal accident, he called me to check how I was doing, as I had injured my back a few months before. I had been recovering well and we enjoyed our usual catch-up chat. I have often wondered what prompted his timing to ring me the night before he died.

It was hard to believe my angel had gone. I did my own little ritual with candles to send him off. Something happened a couple years ago, when I kept thinking of him. I was doing my morning yoga with a candle burning and I could hear it crackling. Looking up, I saw it was out of control, burning wide and high out of the candle holder. Concerned it was going to damage my little table, I watched it for a moment. I thought was someone trying to contact me, by getting my attention? Then I felt I needed to tune into my heart, to receive a message. Immediately I thought of Jason. I'd been thinking of him for the past two weeks, so he must be around me. I asked, "Is that you, Jason?" and I got a beautiful feeling around me, like a warm hug and a message. Yes, he was still with me and was letting me know. Then the candle went back to its normal burning size. What a beautiful gift of love to feel around me and in my heart space. I had goose bumps, which is one of the signs my soul gives me when it is my truth. I felt blessed in that moment.

Jason was my first romance and we had a wonderful adventure together, so many explorations and so many magical experiences. He was an extraordinary soul to have journeyed with in my life, yet I knew I would not marry him, contrary to our families' expectations. He allowed me to open my heart to new experiences and I trusted him. He was also very protective of me, which made me feel he was more like a brother to me as we grew older.

We did get engaged for a short time, but I started to feel him limiting my freedom and would find myself being triggered with angry outbursts toward him, just like I did toward my mother. I realised my free spirit could not be contained, not even by Jason, who adored me. As I became more confident in myself while working as a nurse, my heart began telling me our time as a romantic relationship had ended. We split up just before I left to travel overseas. Two years later, Jason married a lovely woman and went on his own journey, but we always kept in contact with one another.

What do you remember of your teenage years?
Did you have any angels?
Have you ever taken a leap of faith? Where did it take you?

I took a leap of faith and travelled overseas the first time without Jason. I was only sixteen years old. I always felt my journeys inside of me when my heart called me. My heart was palpable with excitement to be going, then fear would arise, thinking *I have no plan*. I did know a family in New Zealand would pick me up from the Auckland airport, but the rest was a mystery. I had only met the family once in Australia when I was very young and had no idea what to expect of them as hosts. Luckily my excitement was too much for me to be thwarted by my fears.

I flew across the Tasman Sea from Sydney to Auckland, New Zealand, so excited for my first air flight ever, my heart pumping with joy. This was my first time meeting my grandmother's Croatian family in New Zealand. They had agreed to be my host family for two weeks, little did I know I would never be the same after I returned. I really felt the love and acceptance of my beautiful aunty and uncle and my three cousins, Danny, Amelia, and little Nadine. I knew straight away in my heart I had done the right thing by going to see them.

Cousin Amelia was one year my junior and Danny was one year older than I. Danny had his car licence and offered to take Amelia and me on a two-week road trip to many beautiful locations in the North Island of New Zealand, like Rotorua, Mount Tongariro, and small towns. I could not stop taking photos! There were many fields of sheep on very lush green hills, mountains and beautiful coastlines to admire; it filled my senses and heart with joy and beauty. My heart was full of love and excitement to be on that journey with my beautiful cousins.

They were so generous showing me their home country, all the delightful beauty New Zealand had to offer, I could not thank them enough. Being the same age group made it even more exciting as I felt true freedom for the first time. I was quite shy at that age, and remembered being in awe of all the freedom they had been given, I had not experienced that with my own family.

I had travelled without Jason, as I felt in my heart that journey was for me to go alone, to meet Grandmother Theresa's family across the water. I could not explain why, it was just a knowing I had in my heart to find my roots with family I had been told about. Jason totally respected that, even though I knew he really wanted to go with me.

Looking back, I was beginning my journey of finding the pieces of the puzzle to my family roots. I still feel immense gratitude for my New Zealand family for giving me a wonderful and memorable experience of a loving family, and showing me the freedom and beauty to feel all my senses. My heart was so open for that first journey outside of Australia. I just knew this was going to be my life journey, a traveller of many lands across the oceans, and now I write this book after travelling all my life to many stunning lands across the planet.

What happens when your heart calls you to travel,
but the plans change?
Have you ever been called in your heart to go somewhere,
but it never quite happened? What did that feel like for you?
Did you do it later?

In my high school days, I had a plan to see the world with a few of my school mates, but their lives changed after leaving school. They found boyfriends, jobs, and other commitments, so travelling overseas was no longer a priority for them. For me it was a heart calling I could not ignore, travelling was my dream and it would come true. Living an ordinary life was not for me. My uncle's slide show inspired me to visit those wonderful worldly destinations in magical lands, and my art studies and teacher had also inspired me to see the world. I knew my life was about finding my freedom, exploring this beautiful planet, and there was another purpose for me. I always had that feeling of being *Alice in Wonderland*; everything was an adventure, with interesting people to meet and new lands to explore.

Some years after leaving school and working in different secretarial jobs, which did not keep my interest — as I would finish projects quickly and very easily — I needed a more stimulating job. One of my bosses suggested I would be suited to do more studies in another career, as I needed more stimulating work where I could learn more.

Starting my new career in nursing, I found many of my colleagues were keen to go travelling with me, so I started collecting ideas on how I would travel. As we came to the end of our training, my friends were all meeting their life partners and I was being invited to weddings, then they were thinking of babies and families, or further study for career opportunities. I thought, oh no, they are not coming travelling with me! Those friends were under twenty-three years old when we completed our three-year Registered Nurse training, and all I could think of was the world was my oyster, my heart and mind were open to new experiences, and I was fearlessly going to find my adventure and freedom, or anything else that was there for me to find.

I was going alone if I had to. Marriage and having children were not on my radar, even though I had a boyfriend I loved very much. Marriage just did not feel right for me. I had watched my mother waiting on my father in many ways and decided as a child that I would not be in that sort of partnership — it would be equal or not at all. I always had a strong passion for the rights of women, children, and animals. I felt justice was needed, as they seemed to be exploited on this planet in many countries and in many ways. This was a time when women's rights were becoming a force, and I would always have something to say about women's rights! This often got me into trouble with my parents' conservative thinking. They married in the 1950s, when most Australian women stayed home and men went out to work and expected to be cared for by their wives who stayed at home.

That older style of relationship did not inspire me in any way. I wanted a partner who accepted my career choices, where we would be equal in our relationship, not divided by women's and men's chores. A little ahead of my time perhaps, in the late 1970s, but some of us were making a path for the young women who come behind us today. I remember older women saying, "You will regret not having children." Now, at sixty years young, I have no regrets. I have lived life from my heart's desire, the one my soul knows well, guiding me to find joy.

I loved nursing because I loved biology and learning about the science of the body and its workings. I loved Reader's Digest books as a young teenager, but I read only the monthly chapter "My Body." I was fascinated to see how the body worked and the function of each organ, so I followed my heart and passion to learn about the body. The bonus was I found freedom to move around and be financially independent, not needing to rely on a husband. I accepted that I could be single all my life, and that was totally fine by me, as long as I could have my freedom and follow my heart.

In the past, Mum told my boyfriends that if they became possessive of me, I would feel my freedom restricted and would not be interested in them any longer. It surprised me that Mum shared that about me. Free-spirited with freedom had always been paramount to me, from early childhood. But why? Was my mother always holding me back? As a mature adult, I have come to believe the strange restrictions Mum placed on me were her own fears projected onto me, which pushed me further away.

I lived in the same neighbourhood until I was seventeen years old, then I could not wait to move out of the nurses' quarters and moved into a flat with Jason before ending my training. My father was silently very unhappy with me and talked to me even less than usual. This went on for many weeks. I had to ask my mother what was wrong with Dad. She said he thought it was very immoral that we were living together and not married. Not surprising, given his conservative ideas around marriage and men and women's roles in society, but it left me to deal with the awful feeling in my heart that I had disappointed my father, the one I so loved in my life.

My heart was calling me on journeys to explore the world, so I just had to overcome those feelings and get used to it, trust it would all be good again with him soon, and live my life as my heart called me.

My father had said, "You will not make the nursing training, you are too sensitive, you will not be able to stand the tough stuff, like vomiting and bed pans." Luckily there is more to nursing than bedpans and vomiting! Dad had no understanding of what was involved from the nurse's perspective, he had only been a patient. His comment was like a red flag to a bull — I was going to succeed at nursing no matter what he thought. I will prove to him I can do this. I guess when I look back, I have never really been a victim, as I always see opportunities to learn.

Nursing training was the beginning of me finding my confidence after being so shy and over-protected by my family; it gave me a real sense of responsibility. I felt empowered, free, and my heart was happy being responsible for helping people.

12

True to My Nature

Before I departed to live overseas at twenty-one years old, I felt some sadness and confusion around leaving ones I loved. But my heart was calling me on a new journey in life, alone.
Have you ever felt called to go to another place to live, many miles away, but also felt the sadness of leaving the ones you love behind?

I loved Jason, but my calling to travel, deep in my heart, was all I could listen to. I didn't know where I would go or for how long, but I was going to the United Kingdom, where my father's family originated. It was the gateway to Europe, and I didn't have a return ticket to Australia.

Something else overshadowed my excitement before I left Sydney Airport.

Have you ever had all your plans turned upside down before you took a big trip, making you wonder if it will ever eventuate?

A phone call, two weeks before I was due to depart for the UK, overshadowed my journey and changed everything for my departure. It was a dramatic turn of events for the whole family.

My sister, Kim, had already left for overseas on a four-week, under-thirties group tour through Europe. Her friend Naomi, who was travelling with her, called to say Kim had been badly injured in a motor bike and bus accident — she was in a Greek hospital and may need to have her leg amputated.

All we could say was, "What did you say? What? Where?" before the call ended. Naomi was using a payphone in a foreign country. It was in the 1980s, no mobile phones then.

My exciting travel adventure was now about going to save my sister. From the vague location Naomi had given us (an island in Greece) we did not know what to do or where to go to find her. Neither I or my parents had ever been to Europe, so we had no idea what to do. The tour company Kim travelled with, Contiki, never contacted us to advise she was sick, and the insurance company found a loophole and decided it was not within their terms and conditions, so refused any assistance or compensation.

Someone in the family suggested we talk to the Australian embassy in Australia and check if they could talk to the embassy in Greece. Mum contacted the embassy in Canberra, then we finally had some action to investigate the situation. They wired Mum and Dad back, recommending Kim be airlifted to London and my parents pay the Greek hospital a substantial amount of money to release her. We still didn't even know where in Greece Kim was! The embassy advised she would need several seats of the plane for a stretcher. That sounded seriously bad, from our limited information. As time passed, the messages were getting even more disturbing, and the situation was sounding seriously worse every time we talked to someone.

Communication was very slow in 1980 compared to today. We had no computer access, only land-line telephone, telegraph, and fax. We finally received more details from the Australian Embassy in Greece, so we knew where she was. The embassy suggested we not go to Greece, but rather meet Kim in London. She was due to arrive in a couple of days, giving me time to leave Australia and arrive in London to meet her flight.

We received very sketchy details on the phone from her friend; she did not have long to talk as it was expensive to call us, and I think we only heard from her on two phone calls. My parents were beside themselves trying to work out what to do.

I had to take responsibility, even though I was inexperienced in life and my plans were changed.
Have you ever had to take on responsibility for others in your family, even though you did not feel prepared?

With Mum's anxieties and fears, I felt she would make the situation worse. Mum was also scared to go on a plane. Dad's lung disease meant he was in no condition to fly. The finger of responsibility was pointed squarely my way. I was the most logical person to go. With my new nursing qualifications, I could at least assess what the real story was with her health status and report back to my parents.

We still needed to confirm with the embassy if they could fly her to London to save her leg with more advanced medical treatment. The catch was my parents needed to wire a substantial amount of money to the Greek authorities before they would release my sister from the hospital and onto a flight that had room for a stretcher. It was peak tourist season, so the flights were full and the money seemed to take a long time to reach the Greek authorities, even though it had been sent promptly. It was all emotionally crazy for everyone, made worse by such limited communication channels.

I had to miss my nursing graduation event and change to an earlier flight. When I was leaving Sydney for London, we finally received a message from the embassy that Kim would be in London within a few days, meaning I would arrive in London in time to meet her. That was good news.

Saying good-bye to all my family, my boyfriend, and friends, I thought how strange, I love all these people, but I cannot stay here with them. I had to go. It was an emotional, bittersweet time in my life.

I cried all the way until the short stop in Malaysia, knowing that I would not be back for a long time, or when — even if — I would see my family and friends again, even though I trusted it would all work out.

Malaysia, the tropical vegetation, the scents of exotic spices and flowers, changed my mood. Excitement was building again—I was on an adventure! I could only think how lucky I was to be travelling abroad.

When I finally got to London Kim was not yet there. I rang the hospital every day, then finally after about a week of waiting Kim arrived. Because she needed several seats of the plane for the stretcher, they had to find a flight suitable for her to travel on to get out of Greece, then they were waiting on the money, which I didn't understand as my parents had sent it very promptly when asked.

The situation was very emotional for everyone. I was in a strange city, not knowing anyone or where to go. My parents were not hearing from me on the phone, as it was costly and I had nothing to tell them until Kim arrived in London. During Kim's flight, another passenger noticed her severe pain and delirium. He happened to be a doctor, so he kindly offered her strong pain relief. Unbelievably, the Greek hospital had not provided her with any medications for the flight.

My sister does not remember much about the whole experience, just that she was screaming at the doctors in Greece not to cut her leg off when they mentioned it would be necessary. Imagine being in that situation and in a strange country where you do not speak the language! No wonder she does not remember very much about that traumatic time.

We learned that the local Greek island hospital was not one you would choose to go to as a patient, as they had limited medical facilities and supplies, and the relatives of patients took food in for them. So, no relative, I guess no food? I think my sister's friend must have taken her food (she continued her tour once Kim was flown to London).

I was at the hospital to meet Kim when the ambulance arrived at the Accident and Emergency (A & E) department. Her leg was bandaged and a serious, severe infection was raging, with gangrene and pseudomonas bugs. It was toxic. The Greek doctors knew it was surging through her body, causing her to be septic. With no medications, they could do nothing but take the leg off to stop the infection from causing more damage, as you would see in the old war movies.

I was there when the A & E doctors were assessing her health status and the seriousness of her condition — how bad was she really?

As a registered nurse, I was very upset by what I saw and had to leave the room without my sister noticing. The stench from her leg was so bad it filled the corridor. If you have smelled rotting flesh, you know it and you never forget it. Her leg was seriously infected with the sickly, unmistakable smell of gangrene, so much so that the medical officers and nurses were trying not to react during the assessment.

When they unwrapped her leg, we discovered it was missing all of her thigh muscle and green mush covered her wound. We couldn't see any blood supply; that was especially bad news. It was an horrific wound. I have seen some terribly bad wounds in my nursing career, but this was up there with the worst. The foul-smelling dead tissue, looked like a shark had attacked her. From the looks on their faces, everyone in the room knew it was serious.

Within one hour they prepared Kim and transported her to the operating theatre. She screamed at me all the way down the corridor, "Don't let them take my leg, Deb!"

I kept reassuring Kim that they were not amputating her leg, they were going to save it. For three consecutive days she was taken to the operating theatre and placed under general anaesthetic while doctors worked to cut away dead tissue and save what they could.

After three days of anaesthetics, her kidneys began to fail. No further surgery could be done until the infection was under control, which meant massive doses of antibiotics. She was quite delirious. I wasn't sure she could feel anything by that stage, with all the poison in her system. I thought that not feeling anything was a blessing. Even to this day, Kim struggles to remember what happened as she was traumatised, as you could imagine.

It was a difficult time for me as well. I was staying at an old, cheap hotel in Piccadilly Circus in London, which was not as exciting as it sounds! It was near the hospital, and I spent all day, every day, at my sister's bedside. I lived on McDonald's takeaway food because it was cheap, which I will never do again! I became so constipated from that terrible food.

I also had a bad experience that scared me. Two friendly young men tried to coax me into their car, around the corner at McDonald's in a nearby laneway. I crossed there every day; they obviously had been watching me and knew I was alone. A young female tourist, very naïve, they came over to befriend me with fancy words. My gut instinct was giving me signals, do not stay here, run! I did, into McDonald's. That was scary and shocked me into not trusting any young men.

Feeling unsupported and fearful, but you keep going.
Have you ever had those feelings of abandonment, feeling alone
and unsupported in an unfamiliar country?

After that event, I called my ex-boyfriend, Jason. I was feeling alone and emotional in that big city. I did not tell him about the young men trying to get me in the car. He had planned a trip to the UK before going to Europe for his holidays, so within a few days he arrived in London to meet me. I still chose not to tell him about my scary event, as he was always very protective of me, like a big brother, and would have probably gone looking for the young men. That would have meant trouble for everyone.

I now know why this event triggered me with so much fear, right to the core of my being. I have since had a memory return from my childhood, an event where I experienced feeling abandoned and danger around me.

I didn't tell anyone about that day, or how much it scared me. I had a reality check — I was alone, had never been to London before and so far away from my family and friends, and this was *not* the adventure I had been thinking of having, any more than my sister's hospital experience. I kept thinking *my sister is sick and I need to take care of her. I cannot let this feeling take the focus away from my responsibility to care for Kim, to keep her motivated to keep healing.* I knew Kim was struggling and afraid without our parents' support in a foreign country, and our contact with them was very limited.

My father's best friend had a relative in London who worked with Qantas. The couple were my parents' age, husband and wife. Our family asked if they would visit my sister and me at the hospital. A lovely, caring couple, we found them to be very supportive. They came in a few times for short visits, which helped me feel someone cared about us. I could talk with them easily, and they had a house and were living in the greater London area.

When my sister had recovered enough to fly home to Australia, I stayed with the family for a short time when I needed a base near London. They always made me feel like their home was my home, like I was their family. They were our angels, compassionate and helpful. Another gift I received was short term accommodation with one of the nurses looking after my sister. This helped reduce my costs for accommodation while I was waiting for my re-scheduled Europe tour to start.

Before my sister was flown back to Australia, she had to learn to walk again. After not walking for so long she became very weak and a physiotherapist was required. I remember the day she first walked with the physiotherapist. I watched with Jason as we encouraged her to take her first steps with special crutches for her legs, her muscles so weak she could not hold her weight. To save her leg, doctors had cut most of Kim's muscle tissue away from the bone. Now they were trying to get her ready for the long flight home to Australia. She had very new skin grafts to her legs which had never been done before (it looked like basket weaving), and it was a last attempt to save her leg.

After some weeks my sister was flown home to Australia and went to Prince Alfred hospital for follow-up treatment, where the specialist doctors were very interested to see her skin grafts, which had not been seen in Australia before either. She slowly recovered, after staying with our parents for twelve months, before moving on to another travel journey. She was not going to let this accident define her as having a limitation; she always believed she would travel again.

However, the accident has sadly changed her life forever. Kim arrived in Australia after all the hospital stays with several blood clots in her body and was told she could not have children—which she ignored! She went on to have two beautiful girls, now young adults. I was at both births and felt honoured. With her second birth she used self-hypnosis, which was quite revolutionary in 1991. What an extraordinary event to witness, peaceful and calming, on a bean cushion on the floor as she sat in a meditation Buddha pose.

Initially, the first pregnancy became a challenge for her to find an obstetrician; many would not take Kim on as a patient, as she was viewed as too risky with all the clots. After searching, she found an awesome obstetrician of Italian descent who believed it was a woman's right to have a child and it was a natural cycle of life. Bless the Italian doctor!

The challenges have continued from the permanent damage of her scarred leg, with lymphatic problems and infections all her adult life. However, it has taken her on a whole new life journey into natural healing therapies and quantum vibrational healing practices that have been revolutionary in helping her and her clients raise their consciousness on this planet.

Thank you to the doctors in London who saved her leg, allowing her to do the great work she does with clients. Bless those doctors for their skills and determination.

13

Dreams Happen

With my beautiful sister safely home in Australia, the dream travel journey I had nurtured all my life became reality and the magic began. I met awesome young people, all around my age (early twenties) and excited to be exploring the world. From many nations, we came together on a wild tour, travelling for more than two months in a big bus, camping across Europe. This gave me the confidence to travel around Europe on my own later, backpacking.

After the tour, I found a flat with gorgeous Australian girls from my tour who were going to work and live in London. They came from regional Queensland and taught me much about the Australian outback with colloquialisms I had never heard — and they knew how to party! I treasured their friendship and we are still in contact more than forty years later.

I worked with a nursing agency and was offered a live-in job as a private nurse for a well-known aristocratic family who had suffered from a politically sensitive event reported on by the British media. Part of my job was to keep the press away from my patient and observe his neurological state when he returned home to the family estate after his hospital stay.

He had sustained severe head injuries from a car accident. His personality had changed as a result, and his memory was vague to the point he was challenged to remember even his name. This had been a very controversial accident, as my patient had been having a romantic relationship with an older married woman, who just happened to be a well-known parliamentarian's wife, so a public figure in the UK. On the day of the accident they were travelling together in my patient's sportscar when he flipped the car. Sadly, both sustained serious, life-changing head injuries.

I was employed to live with the family on their beautiful grand estate, to observe my patient's mental state and report back to the neurologist, as my patient had been very traumatised mentally and physically by this event. It was also my job to keep him safe on the property, as he would sleepwalk and become confused at times.

A newly qualified registered nurse, I had no experience in mental-health nursing, as I had been working in General Nursing surgical/medical wards. At the time I was only twenty-one years old; my patient was thirty. Prior to the accident he had been a successful merchant banker in London, but now faced a long road to recovery.

This was a whole new experience for me, I had never been involved with aristocracy before. I was intrigued by the differences of culture between the aristocracy and my own working-class family in Australia and felt very honoured to have this cultural experience. I remember the first day they picked me up from my London flat — rolling up in the Bentley automobile with a driver to take me out of London to their estate home. The family also had a castle in Wales and apartments in London. I nearly cancelled the assignment, as I felt out of my depth on a cultural level and with my limited nursing experience. I have to thank my flatmates, for they encouraged me to go. I soon relaxed and took it on as another adventure.

That uneasy moment when you feel you may be out of your depth or comfort zone....
Have you ever had that feeling where you've jumped into the deep? What did you do?

Keep swimming!

When I first saw the magnificence of the family estate and was introduced to the staff I felt very apprehensive, but it was soon clear my fears were unfounded, as family members were very kind to me. I settled into my new position easily and enjoyed it, and had regular days off to see my flatmates in London.

I was placed in a room near my patient on the second floor. His mother, Lady J, was also on the same floor. Her husband, Lord H, was living elsewhere at their family castle with his mistress. Those cultural norms were intriguing. To have a mistress openly mentioned to me, and to know Lord H had an open relationship with his mistress at another residence and it was all totally acceptable to the family — in my culture that would definitely be frowned upon.

The difference was again highlighted when I needed background information on my patient's pre-accident activity levels and mental state. When I asked Lady J about her son, she promptly referred me to the family nanny, who had looked after the young adults in the family since their births at the estate. She was quite elderly and still lived on the estate in separate accommodations.

I soon realised that in that aristocratic culture the mother does not really have much contact with her children. I observed that Lady J had a busy schedule at charity and social engagements, sometimes with royalty such as Queen Elizabeth. The family unit, as I knew it, was not the same in this class culture. We had drinks on the terrace every evening and ate in the main dining hall at a huge, carved wooden table. It held many seats for large banquets with the best silver laid out, housed in a massive wooden-walled room, probably oak.

An antique dresser across one end of the room held all the silver cutlery, laid out on top for each meal. This type of formal dining was not how I ever had my meals! I had to sit and observe how everyone used their cutlery so as not to look silly, as I had never used so much cutlery for one evening meal! In the evening we would go to the drawing room for port after dinner. There were kitchen, garden and cleaning staff who cared for the estate buildings and the large open grounds, including delightful old mill gardens and pheasant pens.

I felt the family did not know how to fit me into their class system, as I was from Australia and did not have an identified accent to categorise me into a class system as the English seemed to. So, they just treated me as an equal, and I ate dinner with them in the dining hall and listened to the day's sharing. They spoke mostly about the banking system of the world. I was unable to contribute to that subject. I had only a few pounds in my bank account, so I just sat and listened curiously to what excited them in life. The nanny and the other staff members had their meals in the less formal area of the working kitchen, where we would have breakfast each day.

I received a letter when I completed the contract, informing me the family were very pleased with the care I provided to their son, as was the neurologist with the standard of my professional reports. So much so, the family wrote a beautiful recommendation letter to the nursing agency, stating my good work.

I was in the UK when Lady Diana and Prince Charles were married. I had been offered a private nursing assignment, and on the day of the royal wedding was working at a beautiful apartment with the elderly Lady Eliza. She was very kind to me, and we enjoyed watching the very ceremonial wedding day in the UK together from her apartment window. Little did I know we would have full view of the wedding party travelling past on their way to Westminster Abbey! I did not feel I was working that day. By then I was beginning to really enjoy my time in London, after that stressful start with my sister's illness.

Finding the humour and love in life's moments of confusion and craziness was important.
Are you able to find humour in the craziness that surrounds you at times?

Another of my private nursing contracts was looking after a wealthy lady with a type of dementia called Sundowners, where the symptoms become noticeably worse late in the evening and overnight, after the sun goes down. The family needed a nurse to stay with their mother overnight due to her overnight confusion and living alone. I spent much of the night redirecting her actions. First night, I was sleeping after making sure she had gone to bed, when I was awoken by the washing machine banging and crashing in a cycle, making a hell of a noise. My patient had put all the pots and pans from the cupboard into the washing machine — not the dishwasher! This was the beginning of many nights I needed to find the humour in life's experiences. I knew I was not going to be getting any sleep at this job!

My patient would pack her bags at night for her holiday and try to leave the house. I had some busy nights keeping her safe in the house, trying to stay ahead of her next move. I had to turn off all the power every night and be very vigilant. In the day she was a very sweet little lady, bless her, who was happy and orientated in the house, doing her own thing.

This was just one of many interesting experiences I had in London working as a private nurse. Even though I needed to work to travel, it had to be in my time, so I could travel backward and forward to Europe and the U.S. I did find the balance of work, play and travel.

My husband, originally from the UK, once said to me, "You have seen more of Europe than I did living in England for thirty-three years as a citizen of the UK!"

My response, "I don't like to miss an opportunity to travel!"

*I was finding my way to the freedom I had only dreamt of.
Have you found freedom in your life? If so, how did you?*

Travelling across the world I found my own sense of freedom, which had been calling me for so long to so many new places. Living and working overseas for two years, I met many beautiful young people my own age who travelled with me across Europe and the UK. One such journey while I was living in London was backpacking across Europe and staying on the Greek Islands, where I camped on a beach, wore minimal or no clothes (or a bikini bottom if we felt too naked).

*My experience with my sister's accident did not hold me back
from going to Greece. All fears aside, I was going
to explore Greece for myself.*

The island was inhabited by Greek farming families. Only a small number of backpackers knew of it, and the locals did not seem to mind us being tucked away along their foreshores. "Plenty of space!" I would hear them say.

This was not a tourist island in Greece, but many backpackers were starting to tell others of this little paradise, so it probably is now! It had become a very alternative community; some of the farmers would arrive each day on their donkeys with fresh and dried fruits for us to purchase at very nominal prices. There was a fresh water well behind the beach that we used as our bathing area. Using a bucket, we would take the water from the well to wash the saltwater off our bodies after our day in the Mediterranean waters.

We made little huts from local dried palm branches to keep the sun off us, and the sand was our floor. These huts were dotted along the beach in many shapes and sizes, it depended on what you created out of what you could find. My friend Alana and I had our hut high enough off the ground to sit under and place our sleeping bags underneath, and other people created huts with standing room. It was free-form individual design, I loved that.

One morning, I had just started to wake with the rising sun and was bathing my face in my little hut when I heard scratching.

"What is that?" I asked Alana, just as a big, dark-coloured bush rat ran out past us where we sat contemplating a beach swim to wake up. The sight of that rat woke us up promptly! We quickly checked our food — he had been in there eating our fresh food supplies. I think he must have been there most of the night. That did not feel so good! But that was life in the great outdoors. We laughed it off and it didn't change our feelings for the great location.

It was a wonderful place to be as a young person who loved her freedom, the beach, community, friends, and fresh raw food for our rat friends. Many of the other backpackers were from Sweden, Germany, South Africa, France, and my new friend Alana was from Australia. Such beautiful memories of those times as I travelled around Europe as a free spirit.

Feeling that freedom without family judgments and finding your own gut instincts.

I was in such a blissful place, free of my family's opinions and limitations, finding work when I wanted or needed to, and making new friends at every turn. This is where I really developed the confidence in trusting my gut instincts, as that was all I had to keep me safe; coming from my over-protective Australian family I was still somewhat naïve in many ways.

My insight here:
Later I realised I was not only tasting freedom there, I was learning to trust my own gut instincts for survival on this crazy planet. I believed my instincts would keep me safe for the rest of my life here on earth, something I feel could have been encouraged by my own family when I was growing up, listening to my own intuition to know what is right for me. I felt this quality was not honoured in my childhood, with the disempowerment I experienced.

Have you ever had those experiences where you had to rely on your own gut instincts to find your way through unfamiliar territory? What was it like for you?

One trip I travelled into Turkey and visited the Grand Flea Market and Blue Mosque in Istanbul, where I experienced something that scared me into always listening to my own gut instincts. I was travelling with two very fit, good-looking young South African men, and stepped into the flea market to explore as a tourist.

I was tempted into a little shop selling beautiful Eastern jewellery. My two male companions had not noticed me step off the path and continued walking. I found myself inside a little, dark, flea-market stall. A Middle Eastern man encouraged me to look at more jewellery behind the counter, then invited me behind a curtain.

My gut feeling was starting to stir and I had some doubts, so I continued to just mull around the stall. My two male companions had noticed I was missing, so while I was naively being drawn into the dark little market stall, they were looking for me. My instinct told me to be cautious, so I would not go behind the curtain.

At the same moment a man came out from behind the curtain and tried to grab my arm, my companions arrived at the doorway.

"This is where you are Debra! We had to backtrack to find you!" they called out.

The second man, who had tried to grab me, looked perplexed and rushed back behind the curtain, seemingly surprised to see my male companions. My companions grabbed me, saying, "Stay with us! What are you doing here without us? This is not a safe place to be alone as a single female."

I could breathe again, and realised how fast situations can change. I must admit in that split moment I did feel unsafe and confused. However, I believe that day the angels were looking over me, telling my companions to come find me at exactly the right moment!

I felt blessed that day, particularly as I remembered the story my high-school art teacher had shared about a friend who went to Europe and was kidnapped by Middle Eastern men. Is slavery still happening? I was told later it does exist! I believe that woman did escape, but this story came to my mind while this incident was unfolding. I was so naïve in my early days of travelling, what an experience to teach me to use my gut instincts and internal alarm system! I sure did learn how to tune into my gut instincts and feelings very quickly as I travelled around.

Sometimes while backpacking in Europe I slept on the streets and at railway stations, mostly because it was adventurous to do so. Maybe not smart, but I always used my gut instincts to get a feel for the place before I stopped there. There were other backpackers, so I was never alone. One night a group of us found a spot to sleep right near the port where we would get the ferry next morning to a Greek island.

This was not one of our best ideas, as in the dark of the night we had placed our sleeping bags down in front of a docking gate for the ferry. The next morning, we woke to the horrific sound of a truck horn and looked up to see a huge semitrailer parked in front of us, about two feet away. We had lined the width of the gate with all our sleeping bags and blocked the entry into the port, even though the gate was closed. The driver kept blowing that horn in our faces, as though it was yelling, "Hello! Wake Up Call! Move On!" That was my initiation journey into freedom. I had no family opinions or judgments on what I was choosing to do with my life each day. Maybe it wasn't so safe at times, but I had to do it.

Back to London and working with a doubt over my heart. Have you ever worked and lived in another country, away from your original home? Did it excite you with choices that could change your life?

Living in London, some of my nursing contracts were at private hospitals where the wealthy Middle Eastern sheikhs, their families, and celebrities were treated or operated on. I worked a few weeks there and was given the Middle Eastern patients. They had what I would call apartments for hospital rooms, as everything was available to them. I was paid very highly by the nursing agency service and the families also gave substantial tips if they liked the nurse. I found them to be very polite and friendly families who appreciated the service.

It was not surprising to receive 100 pounds as a legitimate tip for my nursing shift to care for one patient. That was a lot of money in 1980 — one day's extra pay. They would often make small talk with me and ask if I would like to go to their country, as they needed good nurses like me to help at their hospitals. My agency at the time was offering contracts to Saudi Arabia, and some of the nurses I had met from Australia were signing up to go.

I couldn't decide, as I found out that nurses had to live in a compound and could not travel alone because it was unsafe for women without a male escort. I was assured nurses would live in a safe compound and travel by limousine to the hospital to work, or to go out. Where would I go if restricted to a compound? I was very curious, as I heard the hospitals had state-of-the-art facilities and offered great opportunities to learn more in speciality areas of nursing. I already knew money was no barrier in Saudi Arabia, but my heart was feeling some doubts and I had my mind on another adventure, a ski holiday in the Alps for two weeks. I decided to make my decision after the ski holiday. My flatmates were going back to Australia, so I was going to need another flat when I returned to London, or I could take the Middle East nursing contract for twelve months.

Excited, I left London for adventure in the Austrian Alps. First day on the coach, I sat next to an Australian tourist, Alexa, who was also travelling across the world without any plans. We immediately bonded, laughing as we shared our stories over the ten-hour bus ride. Alexa had grown up in Australia in a suburb not far from where I grew up, so we had many subjects in common. We were besties from that day on and had the best ski holiday. I learnt how to do downhill slalom racing and we met a couple of lovely young men who kept us both entertained over the two weeks.

When the holiday ended Alexa was going to live in London and had two other friends wanting to share, so we found a flat and the four of us settled in. I was still thinking of my nursing contract offer to the Middle East and feeling unsure, so I left it to the back of my mind until later.

Alexa had an older sister, Sally, a journalist working for a well-known women's magazine in Australia. Sally was coming to London on assignment to interview and write about Lady Diana and Prince Charles. Sally already had an exclusive hotel booked with her husband, who was a well-known surgeon in Australia, but she spent more time at our flat as she found that more fun than being alone in her hotel.

However, there was another reason Sally spent so much time with us. She and her husband had been lovers since they had met at fourteen years old. Married in their early twenties, they were now in their early thirties and had no children. Sally's husband's family originated from the United Arab Emirates, and while she was busy on her journalist assignment he was having a wonderful time in the United Arab Emirates connecting with his roots, visiting and meeting many sheikhs and family members. Sally decided to go to her husband and meet his extended family. She was very upset to find he did not want to go back to Australia and wanted her to live in the Middle East.

The sheikhs wanted her husband at their hospital and had offered him a palace and a fabulous hospital contract — head of a department, in line with his specialty. She had wondered why he was gone so long. As it all unfolded, it did not take her long to see he was being wooed into a life of luxury and women available to him. Sadly, they separated, and Sally completed her assignment in London and went back to Australia.

When Sally came to visit us, she shared what her experience was like as a woman in the United Arab Emirates — all her rights would have no value and be negated. From that information I decided I would definitely not work in those countries. I think it is interesting that I had doubts inside me and had not committed to a contract with the agency, then when I met Sally and heard her story, I knew it was not for me. I believe my doubts were well-founded. I have met nurses who worked in the United Arab Emirates and enjoyed a short-term contract, but had felt the restrictions of living in a compound and were ready to go home after the contract had completed. Restrictions were not for me; I had just found my freedom and was not going to give it up.

DEBRA A. LANSDOWNE

Learning how valuable my instincts are and trusting that was empowering.

Have you ever changed your plans because the family has influenced you to do something else? How did you feel in your heart, making those changes to please others?

This was my journey of freedom and empowerment. I was learning that if I made a bad decision I would have to live with it. I believe when we honour another person's decisions we are empowering them to grow into a stronger, more empowered conscious human being. I discovered there was no better teacher than my own life experiences.

How I cherished the feeling of being able to find my way across the world, on my own terms, at twenty-one. It taught me to trust my own intuitive guidance with confidence and to listen to those gut feelings, as they are alarm signals. I met friends for life, some I keep in touch with to this day. We had a special bond travelling together; they became my family and I learned you can create family kinship across the globe with anyone you meet if you stay open, listen to your own gut instincts and let your heart guide you.

My senses came alive with the new smells, and the beauty my eyes saw and heart felt in extraordinary lands, the kindness of strangers, kinship with other travellers, and the synchronicities that presented when I was in the flow of life. I found being unrestricted, with no plan, gave me more opportunities for magic to come my way. I didn't have much money to travel, but many opportunities presented to me to have extraordinary journeys of joy.

Many of the learnings and experiences to grow and learn about myself and others in the world would have been missed had I been nearer my family and had more contact, because they would likely have influenced me to some degree or placed doubts in my mind — such as the journey to Israel I cancelled because my mum found out. She was very fearful, so I listened to her and did not go, which I regret to some degree based on my friends' experiences there. Israel is one of those places I still need to visit in this life.

When I returned to Australia, even my career opportunities excelled due to my overseas experience, as I'd had many opportunities to try various specialty jobs in London that I would not have been able to try in Australia without specialty training. Back in Australia I was offered any specialty division of the hospital I would like to work — it was my choice! Wow! As a registered nurse with only two years' experience that was a dream come true, it was not what other nursing friends who stayed in Australia experienced.

In London I had been given opportunities to prove myself and gain new skills. My confidence levels had been raised, as the opportunities allowed me to prove myself and what I was capable of, which was often way more than I thought possible!

This just reinforced my determination to follow my own guidance and heart's calling, not to let others sway me from that. No one else knows what my soul needs, and only my soul knows how to get me there safely.

Before returning to Australia, I made a trip to the United States for three months, camping in a van, to see many of the national parks across the north and south of the U.S. I thought it would be great to try to see my sister on the way around. She had healed herself and had moved to the U.S. to travel and live, and we met up in Los Angeles. We had not seen one another since her hospital stay in London, so it was a very exciting, joyful, heart-warming time to see her full of life again and travelling, even though she had some leg deformity and scarring. I had to admire that quality, to keep going on her adventures. She asked me when I was going home to Australia, as I was still living in London at the time. She told me Dad's health was declining quickly and he may not be around much longer, so that was my turning point. I had to go home to see him and spend quality time with him.

I never read that in any of the letters from Mum. Maybe a sign could have been that my father had written his first letter to me, just before I left London. He had never written a letter to me, not ever, he always left the communications to Mum. I remember the letter and how beautifully funny it sounded, his sense of humour so alive. I kept it, the first and last letter I ever received from my father. I held it at my heart, so excited to receive it. I think perhaps he was trying to tell me he was not well, but he couldn't, he just wrote humorous comments about his vegetable garden and failed attempts to be a primary producer.

After my U.S. trip I went back to London for a short time, packed up my flat and returned home to Australia. Dad continued to shuttle in and out of hospital, suffering with his hideous genetic disease as his health deteriorated. I watched him try to be strong, but he was losing to the disease. When he agreed to have an oxygen cylinder 24/7 we knew that was the downturn for him, he had lost his strength and freedom. He loved his freedom as much as I did; we had that in common.

This was not the end, only the beginning of my journeys across the planet. For the next forty years, to this day, I continue to explore the delights of this beautiful earth.

"Travel brings power and love back into your life."
Rumi

14

Body Wisdom and Intelligence

*Do you listen to your own body's wisdom and intelligence
when it is nudging you to take care of it?
Or do you ignore your body's wisdom, and what happens if you do?*

I had been back in Australia only for eighteen months when disaster struck. I was offered a great nursing position in a cardio-thoracic intensive care unit in a major Sydney hospital. I weighed about fifty-five kilos, and the job required me to assist lifting patients post-operatively in and out of bed. Some patients, ex-footballers, weighed up to 100 kilos. As a young, healthy, and energetic female, I never considered that I would hurt myself. I never said no to any job that presented, even though I was lightweight and had a small frame.

I believe I did not honour or listen to my own body's messages. One day I lifted a patient and oops — something had happened to my back. A strange pain struck, then disappeared. I thought I was fine and kept working, but an hour later my back became painful. I was checked by the Accident and Emergency department doctor, who said I had strained my back and needed two days off. I rested, felt much better, and returned to work. There were no occupational health and safety guidelines then as we have in hospitals now. Thank goodness nurses do not lift patients any longer.

I began to find the work physically and mentally taxing, so changed my position to one that had always interested me — a Community Nurse, visiting people in their homes and providing nursing care. I lasted a few months, until one day I assisted a patient to mobilise in his home and my back tensed and went into spasm. I had seriously injured it this time and was forced to leave work to see a doctor.

The doctor diagnosed torn ligaments in my lower back. He advised that I would not be returning to my nursing career ever again. This was a huge emotional blow, as I really loved nursing, I found it stimulating to learn about medicine, educating and supporting patients through the medical system.

The specialist explained the injury had caused permanent damage and would be a chronic problem for me, as it would be weak and there was no cure to heal it totally. I took the doctor's comments on board and went home with the medications he prescribed. I followed his instructions to rest for the next few months, whatever it would take to be mobile again.

During weeks lying on the living room floor at home to rest my back, I had time to think about what the specialist had said, that my nursing career had just ended. I felt disappointed. I had invested so much time in studying over the years, and now it would be of no use to me, had gone in the blink of an eye.

The medical profession wrote me off! I was devastated to find my nursing contract had a clause that meant the Department of Health Services would not be liable to pay me anything, except to send me to their Workers' Compensation Insurance doctor, who assessed me and agreed I was to be paid half pay for six months, then I would have to go onto the national unemployment scheme for chronic disease.

I hired a lawyer to investigate whether I could get any other compensation from the health system for a chronic injury and discovered that nurses across the country were signing these contracts, wrongly thinking they would be compensated by the Department of Health Services for an injury.

Disappointed again! A young single female needing to support myself, I needed to heal myself soon and find a new career. My specialist suggested a short course of physio and prescribed Valium to rest up in the early weeks. As a nurse, I knew what Valium did to people, there was no way I was not going to be addicted to Valium.

As an adventurous spirit full of life, this was very challenging for me mentally and physically. As I rested, I refused to believe what the doctor had told me for the long term. Believing he had gotten it wrong, I decided to prove them wrong. If I stayed debilitated, my adventurous spirit and heart would die. I had lost my freedom, something I had worked so hard to find. I believed I was not here on this earth to have a limited life, I had journeys and adventures to go on. I had to find a way out of my predicament and be different from other patients with this injury. The doctor did not know me and my will power — when I make up my mind I am committed and nothing will stop me.

After three months of lying and resting, I decided to find a way to rehabilitate and find a positive take on the depressing situation I was in. My guidance was to start swimming. I loved to swim, as it always gave me a sense of freedom, but no way could I manage to do any freestyle. I tried floating in the water to see what happened to my back pain. I took it very slowly in a heated pool at the nearby university just once a week, then two days, then three days. A friend gave me a lift to the pool each time. At first, I could barely sit in the car for the fifteen-minute drive.

My partner Corrine suggested a chiropractor who had helped another friend with a back problem, she said maybe the treatment could help me too. My mind thought, yes, that may work for me, but I did not check in with my body. Mine was a different type of back problem with ligament damage and I needed tender care, no pulling and tugging.

Corrine drove me to the chiropractor for the first session. Oh, my lord! That was a bad decision! After the session my pain was worse than when I arrived. I listened to my friend telling me, "It will be better next time, the first visit just disturbed the pain to realign the back." I was a glutton for punishment, so I agreed to another session because I had no other ideas to heal myself quickly. After that I retreated and pulled the plug on that idea, as I started to realise, I may have aggravated the injury site again.

Thus, began a journey to challenge my professional training in the medical system and to go beyond my own fears of financial insecurity and what my future might hold. I was apprehensive.

After all, I now had a chronic medical condition that made me a high risk for employers to take me on for fear of more medical problems developing. My body and heart were calling me to trust my own inner guidance to heal myself.

It was in 1980s, there were no serious rehabilitation programs available in the medical system for back injuries, only a short program to receive physio-therapy in the first few weeks after the injury was sustained, then you were left on your own with medication.

I was very healthy as a child and don't remember being sick. My mother was very keen to provide the healthiest food she could find, and that often meant we ate fresh produce from Grandpop's farm.

In the early stages I had a wonderful physio therapist who picked up on a malalignment in my hips and gave me some exercises to help strengthen my back and hip muscles. I had to go back to using those strengthening exercises again to give me some relief after the chiropractic treatments. The exercises were never going to cure me, but they did give me some small relief. My inner guidance was telling me I should keep up with the swimming, as it was helping me move more freely in the water, and if I took my time building up my muscles, I would keep getting stronger and more mobile.

That feeling when you know you have taken the right action for your mind and body!
Have you ever had that feeling, when you just know it is the right thing for you to do, but you cannot explain it to others?

After some weeks my time in the car to get to the swimming centre was becoming more comfortable and I had more movement in the pool. Each week I advanced the exercises. This improved my mental state, and I was also doing artwork at home, which gave me a sense of achievement. I continued to do this until I could do freestyle swimming in the pool.

Eighteen months later my mind was clear and my body had healed enough to sit at a desk on a kneeling chair. My relationship with my partner Corrine was not working, so I moved to a new house and found a yoga class nearby. This was a blessing, as I found a wonderfully intuitive and experienced Hatha Yoga teacher who ran classes from her home with a small, intimate group of older women in their fifties. They inspired me to be like them when I reached that age; I was all of twenty-five years old at the time. Writing now at sixty years young, I can happily say I did complete my Yoga Teacher training.

The Hatha Yoga teacher offered gentle postures for me to accommodate my back injury, and her compassion and intuitive guidance helped me take my back's healing to another level. I remember clearly how intuitive this teacher was with her hands. When she touched my back, it felt like magic in those hands, and she always touched at exactly the right point to give me relief. Oh, the bliss of those moments, when you just know in your body that it was helpful and healing to receive. That teacher was one of my earth angels, her classes were so nourishing to my mind, body and soul.

While rehabilitating I did some sketching and freeform art, which opened my mind to see beyond what I had thought possible as a job or career option. My injury was taking me on a whole new journey of discovery, as creativity allowed me to see new possibilities and kept me from feeling negative about my situation. I applied for an interior design course, but missed the enrolment date, so I started an evening course in colour and design while I waited for the enrolment date to come around again. I attended each week, and found a building course for women, full-time for six months, which would give me credit for an Interior Design Diploma.

The building course was free, funded as a government grant to help more women get into the building industry. Initially, I was unable to use a chair in the classes due to my back injury, so I sat on my knees with cushions, then tried a kneeling chair to take the pressure off my lower back, which worked. I so loved those courses, as I had always been interested in architecture and design, now I had an opportunity to study it and possibly find work in the industry. I particularly loved the sessions on sustainable building design and environmental passive design with ways to help reduce use of the earth's resources. Those sessions were very forward thinking in the 1980s, but have since become a more accepted way to approach building design.

Have you ever tried a creative pursuit to open your mind to new ideas?

I did try to find work in the building and architectural industry but had no luck, not surprising given my lack of experience in building. But as I was more open to new experiences, I applied for an administration role at an international medical research organisation. They had advertised for a registered nurse as assistant editor for a professional medical reference book. Unexpectedly, at the interview I landed another job, as the director interviewing me liked me. He felt my skill set would be a perfect match as a Research Coordinator/Supervisor within another division, working with doctors in remote areas. Technically I wasn't in a creative role, but it turned out to be because of all the projects I had to create and set up each year.

I continued with yoga and art classes, as they gave me a good balance after using my left brain all day at work, and I found this supported me to be creative at work. This was my first job in two years after my back injury and rehabilitation journey. It took me to a whole new place in my life; I would never have considered a research and statistical role.

I remember my mother's constant criticism; she'd say things like, "Such and such is very smart, you are not so good at that subject." I was told I was not good at math in high school due to my first-year exam results being 52%. One year later we had a replacement math teacher who spoke my language and I achieved 92% for my math exam, but that did not change my mother's negative comments toward me. She kept telling me I was not very smart.

Working with statistical equations I realised I am not bad at math. I had to calculate formulas, which I successfully did, surprising myself. I tried so hard not to limit my opportunities. Even when my negative mind would tell me, you cannot do math, how can you do this job?, I listened to my intuition. Now

I know that all the negative comments passed on to me from Mum were inaccurate, but who knows that as a child? A child sees parents as all-knowing, unless they follow their own intuitive heart guidance beyond the negative talk held inside.

I had much to learn, which was important for keeping me happy and motivated. I was promoted to the Pharmaceutical Marketing Division two years after I started a course in marketing management. I loved the work, as it kept me stimulated and I was learning all about medical research and the corporate world. I needed my medical knowledge to do the job with the World Health Organisation and General Practitioners, so I felt my nursing was not wasted.

I never told the organisation I had a back problem. For six months I continued to use my kneeling chair, along with medicated ointment on my back, and the situation resolved. The injury has not caused me any further problems, but I am always vigilant to avoid aggravating it.

If I had accepted it as my reality when the well-meaning health professionals told me there was no cure, I would have been categorised as having a disability for life and become unemployable. My self-esteem may never have recovered, I think it would have killed me mentally, pulling me into deep depression.

What has been your experience of the medical system where you live?

I found the medical system did not support patients to take responsibility for their healing, even when I was trying to find the best outcome for myself. While nursing, what I observed with patients is that they define themselves *as* the chronic disease. And yet, we are *so much more* than the disease or disability.

Why let a health professional determine who you are and what you're capable of?

I believe we need to support and encourage patients to find their own way forward early in the disease process. They can have the opportunity to find paid or voluntary work and make a difference in their communities, to feel good about their achievements, instead of feeling hopeless.

I found it disturbing to experience the other side of the medical system, and how health professions make blanket statements to patients without realising how debilitating they can be to patients' recovery, mentally and physically, particularly if patients don't have the strength to question what they are told. I felt I was blessed to see past what others told me, and I had the strength to follow my own inner guidance of my body's intelligence. I trusted my gut instinct and acted on it to find my own pathway to a new life using the skills I had already, but imbued with a new way of using them.

The biggest insight I gained was that I am capable of so much more in my life than I or other people had thought — even those who thought they knew me. I believe much of my success in rebuilding my life was because I felt supported by my network of friends and had a compassionate female partner during my rehabilitation journey who never questioned or judged my choices.

DEBRA A. LANSDOWNE

Have you ever ignored what was recommended for you by professionals, followed your own guidance, and then felt empowered?

My insight here:
Finding that I was more capable than I realised made me feel empowered, and that I have great strength within me to move through life's challenges.

The rehabilitation journey was extra challenging for me, as I had to go against my formal training and learn that the medical system does not have all the answers. I learned that other people/professionals do not know me, so I had to go beyond my fears and old belief patterns and listen to my inner voice. I found great strength within myself to move with what my heart and body were calling me to act on in order to heal myself. This became one of my most empowering experiences in my twenties — to follow my own guidance.

Sometimes we don't even know what we are capable of until we are challenged or forced to move beyond what we are being told or fear. I say do it anyway, let fear be the warning but not the deciding factor, and move forward. The fear will dissolve if you give it no energy, as it did for me.

I also found the benefits of using freeform art. It helped me bypass my logical negative mind, opening me to new pathways of thinking and seeing my "limitations" from a different perspective, with fresh eyes and new insights. It was so empowering — I found my own solutions within my own body wisdom and heart. Art also opened my mind to other activities I had not tried before, like yoga. I so love these activities and they are now part of my life's toolbox.

"These pains you feel are messengers. Listen to them."
Rumi

15

Grief: Nowhere to Hide

Have you ever been challenged by grief and suicidal thoughts?
If so, how did you find a way forward?

A day that is etched into my mind, a day I will never forget in this lifetime, was Sept. 3, 1991, at 11a.m. That was the exact time my father left his physical body and passed into another realm of existence. I thought grief was no stranger to me, after losing my beloved grandparents and my furry companions in my younger years. I believe now they were just preparing me for the loss and separation I would feel upon losing my father. It was as if the biggest journey of my life had arrived — how was I to navigate my way through that time of intense grief?

I write this now, twenty-seven years after my father passed away, with great sadness. I remember how my life slipped into a deep, dark hole, and I thought I would never get out alive – in fact, being totally honest, I did not want to get out. My joy and passion for life had packed up and left me alone, feeling empty.

The one person I loved and adored more than anyone else on this earth had left me. Grief is a strange experience; it can take you by surprise and overwhelm you when you least expect it, or it can consume your life with painful emotions.

Grief eluded me at first, because I felt so numb. I also had many distractions to keep me from feeling those heavy emotions, while the real demon of grief hid behind my busy work schedule and the overtime hours needed to make deadlines in a management role. I had no time to think or feel from my heart, as my mind was in overload, telling me, "You've got this grief sorted out, remember you've been here before, you survived it, and you know it will pass." Well, I know now that was a definite illusion in my mind!

In reality, I had been denying my grief and how it affected my mind and body. Eventually, though, my body intelligence decided to wake me up, and I had to listen. My body was slowly collapsing and I could do nothing to stop it. I had to accept, surrender, and embrace the real feelings that wanted to be felt in my heart. I was suffering from a broken, empty heart, and parts of me were missing. My passion for life had somehow slipped away over the months without me even noticing.

It was an extraordinary time in my life. I had no idea what I was going to face as I descended into the deep ocean of emotions and darkness called grief, or how much suffering grief would put me through before I crawled out and found the light again, transformed.

As I sank like a ship in that dark ocean, for a moment I caught a glimpse of light above me. That light kept me from drowning.

It was the compassion of my partner and my furry companion, who helped me find a way to the surface. I realised early on that no one could really help me there, because I was being initiated to find my own way to the light, just as a moth instinctively finds its way beyond obstacles to the light.

Joseph Campbell's work on mythology offers a beautiful story to understand the healing of a soul. The myth is called "The Hero's Journey," and highlights the dark night of a soul's journey when transformation is taking place. This was exactly where I felt myself: deep, deep down in the abyss, contemplating whether to stay, not knowing how to find my way out. I had never experienced such deep depression and darkness. I was forced to surrender to the transformational journey by giving up my work and social life in order to conserve my energy and keep what little strength I had left to find my light buried deep inside.

I found my body to be quite annoying, with continued pain, but without it I would have stayed away from the outside world for much longer than I did. My body began to eat itself away with grief, causing me a lot of discomfort. It wasn't just my mind taking me into dark thoughts; my physical body was dying, as I could not feel my spirit any longer. I had become separated and disconnected from my own spiritual force and all my love and passion.

Grief devoured my life, leaving nothing for me to work with. I felt I was becoming an empty shell, that nothing in life mattered anymore and it had no meaning without Dad being here on earth with me. I could not feel my father's love, or anyone else's. I was emotionally empty, and numb with my sadness.

I found this beautiful poem with so much truth in the words, as I reflect now on this journey.

"Sorrow prepares you for joy. It violently sweeps everything out of your house, so that new joy can find space to enter. It shakes the yellow leaves from the bough of your heart, so that fresh green leaves can grow in their place.
"It pulls up the roots, so that new roots hidden beneath have room to grow. Whatever sorrow shakes from your heart, far better things will take their place."

Rumi

It took several years for me to see this experience as a blessing. I remember the time before Dad's transplant, and later his last hospital admission, where he spent six weeks basically struggling for his life before leaving his body. I visited every day, driving from one end of Sydney to the other on my lunch hour, and after work, to check on him. I was working in the corporate sector at the time in a demanding role with a full schedule of commitments. I am not sure how I got through those stressful days until he passed away.

How did I get through the abyss?

One week after Dad's funeral, I returned to my demanding job, giving me little time to think about anything else but keeping up with my busy schedules. I needed to keep energised, so I consumed lots of coffee, cakes, and sweets to stay awake and alert throughout my long days — until that didn't work any longer. Then I tried expensive nutritional supplements, but they just delayed the health issues that were starting to present from all the stress I was placing on my mind and body as I denied my emotions of grief. I believe those supplements and vitamins only delayed my symptoms and blinded me from listening to my body, causing more problems. The stress I kept unconsciously pushing down into my body had to rise up eventually, and it did — with a vengeance.

My health issues presented as high blood pressure, a kidney infection, extreme fatigue, weight gain, cloudy thinking, anger, and frustration. I was being triggered by the technology I worked with in my office, so my assistant had to help me with technology issues, seeing that I was not coping under the stress.

Weekends weren't relaxing either, as I travelled up to the coast in traffic to stay with Mum. Since childhood, I'd felt the need to protect Mum and had promised my father on his deathbed I would take care of her. Dad had shared that he felt terribly guilty for leaving Mum. Even though she is a very independent woman, I would visit to let her know I was there for her. Looking back, I'm not sure she really appreciated my visits, because she would spend the time criticising me for bringing my furry companion, Charles (a collie cross cattle dog). Charles was well behaved, so I forgave her, knowing she was grieving Dad and her life had changed dramatically.

It wasn't great timing, but I probably added to her trauma when I shared my secret life (more about that later). Mum's life was now in a state of great change, as she was not the caregiver or wife any longer and needed to find a new life for herself. After thirty-five years with Dad, the only lover she had known in her life, she was fifty-four years young and alone. I can say now, many years on, that she enjoys her own space and newfound freedom, making her own choices. I feel proud and happy for her, finding the strength and courage to find a new life.

Have you ever experienced your body calling you to stop and you ignored it? How did that feel for you later?

I ignored my body calling to me, until it collapsed with all the stressors I had imposed on it over twelve months. I started visiting general practitioners (GP) to investigate why my fatigue was so extreme, as I needed to sleep for many hours every day and never felt regenerated. I went to many GPs and specialists for help, but it was early 1992 and doctors knew very little about chronic fatigue or what to do.

I was told by a Genealogist Doctor (one who has specialised in family disease history) that I suffered from a yuppy disease, "… as a young high achiever you are partying too much, get yourself more sleep." I was insulted at his comment and walked out. That was not me — I couldn't stay awake after dinner, let alone go to any parties! My fatigue continued to get worse, until I could not stay awake at all in the day or night.

My sister Kim had read a book on cancer patients with fatigue and suggested I see the author, Dr. Joachim Fluhrer, a German doctor living in Sydney who was using ground-breaking therapies. A GP, Dr. Fluhrer also specialised in complementary therapies and had good success rates with improving his cancer patients' fatigue.

Other Australian GPs did not acknowledge Dr. Fluhrer's therapies, but I believe today he is sought-after overseas, and less conventional Australian GPs use his therapies to help their patients.

I did go, and Dr. Fluhrer suggested I have some unique blood tests not available at the time in mainstream medicine, to determine my adrenal function. He diagnosed me as having severe adrenal stress and chronic fatigue with digestive disorders. The test results showed my adrenal system was in trouble; I had depleted my adrenal reserves and burnt myself out. Maybe I should have been listening to my body's call. To be honest, I was just happy to have a diagnosis, and that someone believed me that something was wrong.

Now I could work on how to heal this problem, but how? There was no actual therapy to cure, other than resting to build energy reserves and intravenous vitamin therapy to support the body's immune system. No one really knew a great deal more.

The adrenals are known as "the glands of stress," as they enable your body to deal with every sort of stress from every possible source. Your resilience, energy, and endurance all depend on proper functioning of the adrenals. The message, loud and clear, was that I had to surrender totally, keep resting, and slowly monitor my activity levels. By slowly, I mean according to what I could manage. There was no magic pill for this, just perseverance.

I became deeply depressed and was considering suicide. I once loved life, now I was sleeping all day, I mean twenty hours! No exaggeration here! I was too tired to get out of bed. I am indebted to my dog, Charles, who sat beside me as I slept.

Letting go of my marketing career was devastating. This was twelve months after my father's death. I was thirty-four years old and had invested seven years into rebuilding my career after my debilitating back injury. Now I had to let go again.

Life with adrenal stress isn't fun for anyone. My partner was giving me breakfast in the morning, before she left home for a demanding corporate job. She returned home to wake me up and encourage me to eat dinner and shower, then I'd go back to bed to sleep. I couldn't even walk my beautiful, loyal furry companion Charles around the block.

My energy and life-force had faded away and I had no stored energy reserves in my body. It was an exhaustion that was difficult to explain. I was experiencing how powerful the adrenal system is. If you have lived with this condition you know that regeneration does not come from a good night's sleep. So much more is needed.

My mouth was full of ulcers, it got so bad that 10% of my tongue was eroded and ulcerated. I lost my appetite and felt I just could not take any more — emotionally, physically, mentally, or otherwise. Forced into total surrender, I crashed into a heap.

My life had been a mission to be free on this planet and a calling to travel, which I had been doing, to all corners of the world, until my father passed away. I needed my life back. I was very frustrated with not having my freedom and feeling unable to live a healthy life.

I visited an experienced naturopath, who was shocked to see the ulcer damage when he checked my mouth. He asked to take photos of my tongue and mouth ulcers because it was the worst case of extreme ulceration erosion he had seen and it was a good case study on digestive-tract disorders for his students. Yes, I thought, if you can help me heal this painful disease that is eating me away. I was happy his class would benefit from my misfortune, but I needed help to heal it. I was living on vegetable juices.

He prescribed some herbal tonics for my digestive tract but unfortunately, they made no difference. I continued to suffer from this excruciatingly painful problem and could only tolerate a liquid diet — and not the alcoholic type! At times, the pain was so intense with some foods that I would feel like I was going to pass out. You don't realise how sensitive your tongue is until it's damaged.

While the adrenal stress was causing chronic fatigue, I was becoming even more depressed — and then I started to urinate blood. I was diagnosed with a severe kidney infection but refused to go to hospital, so the doctor prescribed double strength oral antibiotics, but the pharmacist questioned the dosage and had to ring the doctor to verify. In a few days my kidney infection started to resolve, but my blood pressure was still very high, which worried the doctor. I didn't want to take blood-pressure pills, as I knew my normal blood pressure was low. I felt in my heart that the high blood pressure was due to the kidney infection, which proved to be true. I was malnourished, even though I had been gaining weight, as my poor digestive absorption was not allowing nutrients into my body.

I remembered later how my father died, with many terrible mouth ulcers and many other organ problems as his body shut down. The ulcers had caused him so much more pain and suffering on those last days. I felt I had been literally eating myself away from the inside out with grief. Grief had become my best friend, but it also kept me feeling very depressed. Was that how Dad felt as he fought to stay alive? Dad had always been my hero. He wasn't perfect with his anger issues, but as a child I saw him as the big heart in my small world. I felt such great loss, empty, as though my heart had been ripped out. I didn't want to be here without him.

Even though I had experienced some heated moments in my relationship with my dad, I always felt his heart, his sense of adventure, and loved his humour and stories. Dad was very popular — everyone loved him! He was generous too, often giving gifts to my sister and me. I saw him as strong and physically healthy, until his illness started to erode his energy and happy nature. He really struggled and became frustrated with that feeling of weakness. He would often sit and observe situations with no comment, so I never knew what he was thinking.

Dad and I were both very determined, and his conservative ideas around marriage and family created tension between us at times. As an independent, forward thinking young woman in the 1970s, I did not subscribe to the traditional woman's role in the home. From a very young age I felt my calling to go on adventures, even though I did not know what or where. Something inside was calling me to a different life. My connection and inspiration with Mother Earth have given me a feeling of being different for much of my life.

Have you ever felt you needed to find a way out, but did not know where or how to do it?

I needed to find a way out of the big health decline that was draining me of energy, and it had to be soon to change my depressed mental state. No one was really giving me any clues on how to do this. I'd always had a very active and busy mind in the past, and now I was feeling cloudy and slow to respond with answers.

My sister suggested some relaxation tapes she had made for clients, a short ten-minute technique to calm my busy mind. It did make a difference, but not for long enough. However, I did feel peace in my mind for twenty minutes after completing it and that was a welcome feeling.

Suicidal thoughts were driving me crazy. When my girlfriend Kara went to work, I spent many hours thinking about how I would commit suicide. Kara's mother had committed suicide using the exhaust of a car. When Kara noticed a change in my depressive thoughts I think it alerted her to keep an eye on me. She always took great care to listen to me without judgments and I found that so helpful. She never gave me advice and this felt healing for my old childhood wounds.

My sister's friend suggested I try a Vipassana meditation retreat, to learn deep meditation. The only catch was no talking for ten days and staying in total silence to meditate for ten hours a day. I wasn't sure I could sit without talking for ten days, but what did I have to lose? I was having vibrational energy healing therapy, and the therapist shared after assessing me that many of my chakra centres were barely showing signs of energy flow. No wonder I was feeling tired, my life force was not in a healthy flow.

Do you know what chakras are and how they affect the body?
Have you ever had vibrational energy healing?
If so, did it help you heal?

If you haven't already explored chakras, they originated from the yogic and ayurvedic traditions. The word chakra describes wheels of energy found throughout the body. Seven main chakras align the spine, starting from the base of the spine through to the crown of the head, with many more connected with the body. These seven main energy centres, if out of balance, can affect our health and well-being, mentally, physically, and spiritually. In the 1990s the word chakra was lesser known in Western culture than it is today. Some years after my introduction to chakras I trained in chakra dance therapy and learned how to stay healthy.

The therapist worked on my energetic field every week to balance my chakras to support a stronger flow of energy. At first it helped me immensely and I felt the difference straight away in my body. I felt alive and energised at the end of each session, because it gave me a glimpse of how my old life had felt. Sadly, within two days I was back to that lifeless person with no energy.

How did that happen? I felt so much better, then I felt poorly again. That was a turning point, where I finally realised that no one else could heal me — it was all up to me. If I had the right mindset and the determination to find good health again, I would find a way for myself. I gave the Vipassana Meditation retreat a go and learned serious meditation with no tools — no chanting, music, journals or phones, just me and my mind, experiencing how my mind was controlling me.

I was also detoxing my body with a pure vegetable-juice diet for three months. Unable to eat solid food because of my mouth problems, I was forced to detox with juices. In the 1990s that was seen as extreme by most people, who didn't hesitate to tell me I would get sick. Seriously? How much sicker could I get — my body was getting no nutrients! The detox was rough for the first fourteen days. As I felt the effects of toxins leaving my body, I experienced headaches, flu, aches and pains all over, and more fatigue, but I kept going and trusted in my heart it would work. My energy levels started to improve as my body was finally receiving nutrients, even though my digestion problems had not yet resolved.

Even though I started to gain a little more energy, I was still experiencing a high degree of fatigue. Could I find the energy for the meditation retreat? I read the pre-Vipassana meditation notes, which stated I needed to be well with no mental problems and no drugs. If the centre knew how sick I really was they would probably have made me wait until I was stronger. That was not going to happen, I was going. I had made up my mind. I fudged the form and signed that I was physically and mentally fit.

16

Epiphany and Revelations

My turning point was learning meditation.

*I finally learnt how to take control of my mind
and let go of my busy thoughts.*

Our minds are overburdened with thousands of thoughts every minute, so we can never stop thoughts, but we can take control of what we react to and focus on by becoming the witness, or the observer.

This did not happen easily for me. I had to release and experience all the pain and suffering I had pushed deep into my body, the shadows of the past I had created by my emotional reactions. I needed to be the witness of the sensations that were arising and causing much pain in many parts of my body. Learning to be the witness was very powerful, particularly as I observed how it changed the energy in my body from agitation to calmness.

I soon realised that everything in life changes, that is the nature of life.

The only thing we can know that will happen is change, so why get fixed on a reaction or trigger and cause ourselves so much more pain and suffering by reacting when triggers or negative emotional responses of the mind push us? I learned that reacting usually means avoiding, suppressing, and expressing our frustrations as emotional triggers. The body keeps a record of all our emotional responses, storing them as triggers to be healed. What I was learning at the meditation retreat was not to make more pain and suffering, but to practice being in a neutral, balanced mind when emotions or discomfort in the body arose.

It was one of those ah-ha moments for me, as someone with a lifelong journey of being driven by my emotions. My first three days at the retreat were painful, as I released the hidden pain in my body and delved deeper into my subconscious mind. I was feeling how my body holds negative reactions to my thoughts as a memory of discordant energy that feels like pain. Like little bubbles, these memories get released from the subconscious as you go deeper. Each one has a pain memory in the body attached to it, but if you stay in a balanced neutral mind and bear witness, simply observing the discomfort, it disappears forever. There is no story attached, just a pain memory held in the body's memory.

Your body is like a computer, it holds all the records of your reactions and you cannot hide from it. I learned that our challenge as humans is to practice being the witness to what happens in our bodies. This meditation practice also started to make me very sensitive to the energy in my body, so I could feel so much around me. I remembered feeling those energies as a child, how I could feel the natural world around me, and other people's feelings.

> *"The highest form of human intelligence is the ability to observe yourself and not judge yourself."*
> *Krishnamurti*

The quiet mind gave me space to hear my own wisdom from my soul — that other voice within me was being heard. My mind, body, and spirit started to wake up. I began to feel clarity, and my energy started to slowly improve. I could feel the difference each day. I was detoxing my mind through meditation and my physical body with healthy diet options, herbal medicine to support cleansing — and I even cleansed my colon with hydrotherapy.

I learnt how the colon, our large intestine, stores many toxins in the body before we empty our bowels. Surgeons use colon therapy on patients before bowel surgery so they can see the lining of the colon when they operate or investigate. The difference is, doctors use oral drugs to flush the colon, while colonic therapy uses purified water to flush the colon while you rest on a bed. I believe many surgeons now use this technique pre-operatively, but it was not the case in the early 1990s when I had my sessions. A slow process, it takes about an hour, but can be quite relaxing.

Have you heard of colon therapy? If yes, have you tried it? How did you find the experience?

A strange treatment, I found it highly energising, a feeling that lasted when I left the session each week, so I continued for eight weeks and my energy levels improved dramatically. Friends said they noticed my eyes and skin looked very clear, and that I looked like I'd lost years off my age. I believed it flushed out years of toxic materials stored in my colon, which could have been absorbed back into my body, causing illness.

My insight here:
Some revelations from my meditation experiences at the Vipassana retreat.

I needed to let go of my father and all that he represented in my life, of getting his approval by having a successful, well-paid career that may not have totally resonated with my heart. I had to let go of my old life, now that I had found Who I Am.

My childhood wounds of judgment and not loving myself surfaced to be released, as they were triggering me and blocking me from finding great compassion for myself.

I experienced my body as a vibrating energy force that dances with the unified field of consciousness. I felt this strongly in my body. As I went deeper into the practice, the vibrating force gave me such a strong sensitivity to every other force around me, such as with people and nature. I could not ignore it.

I experienced how we create pain and suffering for ourselves when we react with strong emotions to events, if our mind is not in a neutral balanced space. This disturbs the peaceful, rhythmic vibration of the body, and is then stored as an agitating memory deep inside the body. This distortion is then released at a later time when we are triggered by someone or something in our life, because it wants to be healed to find that peaceful, rhythmic vibration again.

Another revelation was to see into my body and feel the cosmos within me, as a microscopic copy of the outer cosmos that surrounds me, and how we are all connected as the one energy force. These are the cosmic laws of how everything moves and changes, how the patterns are replicated inside us and outside of us, out into the sky above us, into the universe and galaxies. We are a microscopic galaxy. Not sure if I have lost you here, but it was really getting interesting to go deep into the meditation of silence, as the witness.

My next experience may appear to be a drug trip, but I assure you it was not! It was very real for me.

Have you ever had a spiritual epiphany?
Can you remember how it happened and what it felt like?

I had a spiritual epiphany at the meditation retreat. I experienced great bliss and felt liberated from pain and suffering. My heart expanded way beyond my physical body, more than I had ever experienced. I could only feel unconditional love for myself, for everything in my energetic field, and all that surrounded me, including the natural world. I felt part of everything; it became fluid when I moved, as we all moved as one energy force together. The trees and plants all changed to beautiful intense colours, my body was vibrating as it communed with all of nature that surrounded me in the garden where I sat. It was pure bliss.

How did this happen? I was on day four or five of the meditation retreat and in a break session in the garden, feeling my heart opening and expanding, enjoying the natural world and feeling gratitude after the past three days of witnessing my own pain and suffering. As I admired my surroundings, this beautiful, blissful energy spontaneously came out of the top of my head and fell all around my body, into my auric field surrounding me. My body went immediately into bliss. My mind was communing with all nature telepathically.

I felt as though I had left earth and gone to heaven. There was no time, as everything had a fluid feel about it. In every movement I made, I could feel the natural world energy shift. It was extraordinary. All I could feel was unconditional love for everything around me, and it was magical. The intensity lasted until I heard the bell to return to the meditation session. I felt the energy shift, but it did not go away. It stayed with me for another six weeks, then lost its intensity each week as I grounded back into the earthly world of distractions.

Such a beautiful gift to behold . . . I will never forget it. In fact, it is what I aspire to feel inside me again one day. If I keep healing my heart and raising my consciousness, I know this is the place I want to be in my body. The feeling was similar to my experience in the backyard as a small child, when I would sit for hours communing with Mother Nature and observing the little world below me on the grass. I remember I would feel other people's energy around me, I was so sensitive to other people's emotions, but then the intensity changed after a traumatic incident and I lost trust on earth, changing my life on this planet.

I was not naïve, thinking I had become enlightened or liberated after 100 hours of silent meditation. This is something many avatars and masters take lifetimes to achieve, but I do feel confident I know what that feeling is, and I know how to get there, by raising my conscious state and healing my heart and wounds to make space for the magic that awaits us all on this beautiful earth.

I left the retreat in a very sensitive state. Someone could have beaten me up and I would have smiled and felt sad they were in so much pain, sad that they did not know what they were doing to themselves, storing more pain in their body. I would feel only compassion for them. I was so careful not to tread on an ant when I walked in the garden, for I would feel its pain. This was a very heightened sensitivity and showed me what we are capable of as humans. Imagine an earth with everyone so compassionate they do not want to hurt others.

The Vipassana experience helped me to let go of all my attachments, material possessions, and people. If I did not feel that a person or thing was going to help me grow consciously, I let it go. I became a minimalist, but to be honest I didn't own a great deal anyway, as I had moved a lot. I believed I did not need things and could manifest what I wanted in life, allowing the universe to deliver in divine timing if it benefited my soul's growth and learning.

This healing and transformational journey cleared me physically, mentally, and spiritually as I had to surrender and trust the process that unfolded. I feel it plugged me back in to the cosmic force that is in and around us and everything, giving me such passion again and a new life journey to explore, to find who I really am, why I came to earth, and what my gifts are to share. My true purpose in life unveiled itself to me when I was ready and fully open to receive the message.

Have you ever had a challenge that became an initiation in your life and totally transformed you, helping you to see your life and the world with new eyes of awareness? If so, were you ever able to go back to your old life?

My challenge, or initiation, was my grief. I believe the sand inside the shell of my body rubbed me until I had to surrender and break open to release my pearl deep inside. I then found true freedom, self-empowerment, wisdom, joy, and great compassion and love for myself. When I felt compassion and love for myself, I then shared it with others; it flowed freely from me to those I met. I now understood the importance of healing the past pains locked deep in the body in order to expand and raise our consciousness.

I finally acknowledged that my father had given me a gift, a challenge or initiation to find who I really was, and to find a new life for myself. Even though it felt forced upon me to make the changes, it was exactly what I was needing at a soul level. It happened at a very significant time in my life, on my 33rd birthday. In numerology this is the master number, which means it resonates at a higher vibration than any other number. It carries the energy of many spiritual and religious aspects and mystery schools on the planet, as the master teacher, and resonates with mind, body and spiritual growth.

And lastly, thirty-three is the angel number, very spiritual and emotional. I believe my father must have been an angel and he blessed me with a gift, to evolve consciously on this planet to find my own wisdom and who I really am.

> *Did you find any insights here in my sharing of experiences? Have you ever experienced someone's challenging behaviour towards you? How did it make you feel?*

Our reactions to our thoughts are being logged deep into our subconscious in every moment, so we need to be vigilant in how we react emotionally with our thoughts and feelings. Reactions stored in the subconscious mind are like programs that unconsciously keep replaying, by triggering us to react based on the past emotional response we felt for a past event. The mind does not know the difference between new or past events, it wants to attach an emotional memory or judgment from the subconscious mind held in the past.

> *I believe meditation is essential for healthy mind, body, and soul guidance.*

> *Do you meditate regularly? If so, what are the benefits for you?*

My new life included a meditation practice every day to keep my focus and not be distracted by the material world, which I found empty. Meditating regularly is an opportunity to connect with one's soul wisdom and guidance, by spending time in silence, quieting the conversation of one's mind and tuning one in to the timeless peace of the soul's presence. In my meditation, my thoughts pass, without my reactions.

As I began to experience the complete silence in my body-mind, I recognised that I am not my thoughts, but the being who is having the thoughts sent to me. I began to realise I am not my body, but the witness of my life, and I have control over what takes place. I also started to tap into my own wisdom, to gain guidance in my life. I believe when you glimpse the soul in this way you begin to experience more expansive states of consciousness, then you can feel the oneness of all that is.

I love this description of meditation by Yogi Bhajan, Kundalini Yogi Master:

> *"Self-invoked, hypnotic dream, in which you clean your subconscious."*

That is why meditation saved my life. I stopped listening to all the thoughts going on in my "little" mind that caused depression and suicidal thoughts. I started to connect to the unified field of consciousness of all that flows through me and everything in our world. I felt connected and plugged into a bigger force than myself that gave me energy and insights to see my bigger vision on this earthly journey. I felt supported by the universe. No longer separate, I received strong, clear guidance.

17

Secrets Come Out

A secret I had not shared with my family needed to be told after Dad's death, as Mum and I needed to organise the funeral arrangements, which meant her staying with me in my city apartment. That was a little tricky, as only my sister knew I was living another life in the city, away from what my family knew of me. So when my mother came to stay, she was confused as to where she would be sleeping, given that there were three of us in my two-bedroom apartment.

Maybe not the best timing, but I had to let my secret out and be honest with my mother, so I told her I had been living in a same-sex partnership with Kara for three years. Mum was speechless, not sure what to say. Then, as expected, she found a comment to share, "It's just a phase you are going through, it will pass and you will have a boyfriend later."

I was taken aback as she justified my life with Kara as, "just a phase." I felt this was a long-term relationship, we loved one another very much and were very compatible living together; we had lots of fun together. To be fair, Mum had no idea I had been living this same-sex lifestyle for several years, but her response was what she needed to cope with my exposed lifestyle and no more discussion took place that day.

Poor timing perhaps, but I couldn't keep the secret any longer as Mum would now be part of my "other" life, staying in my apartment with my partner Kara and me. Mum and Kara had met on occasions, so they already knew one another and got on very well, thank goodness. I always felt guilty for being compelled to tell her at such a sensitive time in her life, but I felt it was time, and I just had to say it and honour the fact that my partner did exist but not as the opposite sex. Mum was so distracted by the funeral arrangements it didn't seem to make a great deal of difference.

After sharing my secret I felt a weight lift. Previously, I constantly had to stop and think about what I said to my parents, now I was able to speak freely about my life. I had been living a very happy life in the gay and lesbian community in Sydney for some years, with a joyful and supportive network of friends. I loved my life, apart from not being honest with my family and work colleagues. That had been difficult, as I could never share anything about my social life and I avoided the conversation about boyfriends, using my demanding job as a distraction.

I had separated myself from my family, not turning up for family events unless it was a big event like a wedding. In that case, I would ask a male friend to be my partner. I hadn't told my family earlier as I didn't want to disappoint my conservative dad, and with all the health issues he had been experiencing I didn't want to add to the family's stresses and challenges. To be honest, I didn't want to feel judged by my immediate and extended family.

I never fully viewed myself as a lesbian, which challenged some of my friends in my community to engage in lengthy discussions on the use of labels to define ourselves by our sexual orientation. I had enjoyed some lovely male relationships in the past, but none held my interest to be married. I had been proposed to by three different male partners, but I would feel restricted and had to leave them.

I don't think you would choose to live a separate lifestyle from the mainstream, unless you were called to be with a special soul in a relationship. Now I see it has all changed considerably, with everyone coming out and being accepted in the community, but I cannot help thinking it has done a full turn-around as I see signs of it almost becoming fashionable to say, "I am part of the lesbian and gay community." I do remember those early days when we were at the gay and lesbian festival and people were beaten up for attending. I am so glad that is not the case now, or at least occurs rarely, and if the fashion has reduced the prejudicial thinking that is a positive shift.

In the 1980s I found being part of the gay and lesbian community a difficult life at times, because you always had this secret you never wanted to share with others for fear of ridicule and judgment. It was a life that I felt separated me from my family in many ways, and even from mainstream activities within my workplace. I kept it a secret from my work colleagues, except for one woman who I would often see at some of the gay nightclubs I frequented with my friends.

My romantic relationships have never been limited by gender. When my heart calls me to be attracted to a soul (male or female) I follow that calling. I feel and see the soul inside the human bodysuit. I have been blessed to experience male and female relationships, and after finally speaking my truth I have not let other people's judgments and thoughts limit my life. This allowed me to learn so much about myself, from these different gender journeys.

Experiencing very beautiful, deep love — not of this dimension, is all I can describe it as. How can that be, you may ask? Mostly, we do not know the bigger picture of what we are guided by our hearts to do, but sometimes we are given a message later. When I was grieving my father's death and collapsed into a dark hole, my beautiful female partner supported me so lovingly to find my way out of the darkness, without ever judging me or telling me what I needed to do. She just supported whatever I needed to do. I call her one of my angels who came into my life.

Do you find yourself worrying and not trusting in the flow of life? How does that affect your decisions each day?

After my transformation awakening I was meditating daily, as this supported and maintained my strong soul connection. I trusted I would have abundance and accepted things in my life without feeling anxious or competitive, excited to see what journeys my heart would guide me to next. I stopped worrying about everything, and started to trust in my heart and felt light with love and compassion for everyone and all beings. I noticed opportunities and abundance were manifesting for me as I stayed with my soul's calling.

I stopped going on weekend motor-bike rides with my partner, as I lost interest and realised the freedom was coming from inside me. I did learn early in life that I needed to stay light when I move a lot, or I will have to keep dragging all my stuff with me, and that caused stress. However, when I met my partner she had so many possessions it filled our little city apartment. I could not expect her to give up her possessions, it had been my choice to stay light, so I honoured her choices, as she so respectfully honoured mine through my transformational journey.

Within two years of my transformation and letting go of my career, I had a new house to move into, part-time work, and a whole new network of like-minded friends. How did that happen? Kara and I visited our bank manager to advise him we could no longer afford the payments on a little block of land in a regional area north of Sydney. After some discussion, the manager offered us a house loan to build there and leave our city rental apartment. He suggested we could afford the house payments if we could find work in the new location out of Sydney.

It's interesting how when we released possessions and trusted, we manifested abundance with a beautiful new home near the beach, and my partner agreed for me to design the new house. This made me very happy, as my passion had always been to have a house that had minimal impact on Mother Earth. I used all the passive-energy design features I had learned many years prior during my building and design course.

In fewer than twelve months we had relocated to our new home on the coast. I was blessed to be enjoying my time on a large balcony, high in the tree canopy with birds visiting us all day. This area was a wildlife-friendly region, as we were surrounded by national parks and beaches. A job for me manifested locally in our new community and I connected with a new network of like-minded friends. I loved living in the house — but two years later I left the relationship and the house behind.

As my new life journey to continue raising my consciousness evolved, I realised our relationship did not hold my attention any longer. Kara was still living her career in the corporate world and my purpose in life had changed, so my old life no longer interested me.

Even though I still loved Kara, I had new priorities and a new journey calling me. I had to make the decision to leave her, which was not easy. I was fearful too — I was getting older, what if I didn't meet another partner so beautiful and was destined to be alone? I looked that fear in the eye and knew if I did not leave I would be ignoring my heart and would never be happy, compromising my life purpose. So what if I am alone without a partner? It is what it is. Beyond the fear, I knew I would find joy, as I always had. It was time to let go of my fear and see what might unfold. I had no idea where I was going or how I would get there.

The decision to leave Kara was confirmed unexpectedly when a past-life memory came to me of Kara and I when we lived in medieval times. It was very traumatic, and I was warned before this came to me. In that past life, she and I were healers and worked with herbal medicines in a little village. This is not a pleasant vision, but it helped me know I was making the right decision to leave, as we had completed our cycle together and healed our hearts. She was being burnt on the stake by soldiers, and I was being raped by army officials while she burned. I could see all this vividly in my past-life vision.

It was very real when I relived it; I could feel the strong, painful emotions rise within my body and heart when it was being released to heal and open my heart. When I shared this past life with Kara, she totally got it and felt it at a deep level within herself. I believe that from my heart healing, Kara's heart was healed too and we let go of the traumatic memory, releasing us both to move on in our lives. My message was that our time together as souls had completed.

I still remember that first meeting with Kara in this life. It was at a mutual friend's birthday party. Attracted like strong magnets, we danced all night together and did not even acknowledge anyone else in the room until the music ended. We barely exchanged words, just holding eye contact. It was an incredibly powerful knowing at a deep soul level that we had known one another before, in another time. You might see it as falling in love at first sight; I felt it was two souls who knew one another from the past. Many of my relationships have started powerfully at first meeting, then become longer-term relationships, and then I would feel when it was time to move on for my own growth. I don't always have a message on why, but I knew in my heart and it worked for both of us.

Kara was happy living at the new house and had taken up scuba diving, and eventually found another partner. Twenty years later I am sixty years young and can say I found a magical life awaiting me, a magic carpet ride — and it happened because I followed my heart.

Have you ever had feelings for someone of the same sex and felt confused? What did you do about it?

18

Awakened and Conscious Now

Do you know what being more conscious and awake in your life looks and feels like? If yes, what benefits have you noticed?

After rising from the ashes, as the phoenix does to be reborn, I felt transformed, my unconscious life left behind. I experienced such aliveness within me, as if a light had just been turned on inside of my heart, while my body was sensually feeling the world around me. It was a joyful time, I had ascended out of the abyss with my spirit connection and my passion returned and overflowing; it was palpable to anyone who knew me.

So much optimism and enthusiasm, I could only compare to when I was a very young child and found the world a curious and fascinating place to live in and explore. I was having new experiences of a spiritual nature, my physical body felt renewed, and I was told I looked ten years younger than my real age. Life had become a magical place for me to be, here and now. I had forgotten that feeling over the years, as I had become part of the material world, the marketing machine that keeps us buying, then working hard to pay for the things that never actually made me happy or free.

I had found real freedom and totally got it — freedom is within us. I could feel freedom's power and the liberation it gave me. In fact, I felt my soul was the master guide in my life's journey again. I had a new purpose that warmed my heart and it felt unstoppable — I would not let anything distract me from the calling in my heart. As I meditated every day, I could feel my intuition and psychic ability gaining the strength of a lion. My mind had become a sponge, I could not get enough books on metaphysics, spirituality, and ancient earth wisdom. I devoured it all, as if it was my last day on earth.

A journey of a more conscious human had begun in so many ways. I felt I was now living from my soul's purpose and plugged in to the unified field of consciousness, and it gave me passion, strength, and optimism to take this new life journey, learning more about myself and the cosmos around us. My memory of why I came to earth unfolded before me with no effort.

Have you ever seen yourself as a creator or a victim?

I realised I am a creator in my own world, not a victim, and that my outer world is my mirror. If I did not like what was happening in my world I no longer looked outside; instead I would look inside of me to see what I was creating.

It was time to manifest the life I would like from the inside out. I had the tools of a deep meditation practice to support my journey to find the peace and joy within me. I really got it: mind over matter. As my mind found the balance, the physical body was finding a balanced state of being at an accelerated pace to heal itself. I was no longer a victim of my health issues.

In my outer world, I found more magic that surrounds us here on earth every day when we make those deep connections inside within us. I began to believe that being human also meant living in many realities at one time, not just this 3D reality we are told we are limited to. This woke my curiosity to learn more deeply about being a conscious human. I joined groups learning about Ancient Earth Wisdom. These teachings and experiences expanded my heart to heal more, to remember my past lives, and learn new healing skills using my third eye.

No longer confined to 3D reality, I had experienced so much more happening around me and how we affect everything energetically with our conscious or unconscious interactions. My heart wanted to consciously support humanity and Mother Earth, by doing what I love in life and being outdoors communing with nature.

Do you experience synchronicities in your life?

I began to notice many synchronicities and meaningful coincidences in my life. I did not see the synchronicities at first, but then started to recognise people turning up in my life when I was feeling the call to learn more. New opportunities were presenting for my growth to expand my consciousness.

As my spiritual life unfolded, I felt a calling to lead regular meditation groups at my home, and beach meditations on the

Equinox and the Solstice times of the year, to encourage people to feel the joy of connecting with our Mother Earth as I had done.

My sister Kim, myself, and another friend were meeting at the full-moon times. Kim channelled spiritual messages and we were guided to offer regular full-moon meditation gatherings so many other women could experience this powerful time and the importance of connecting with all the phases of the moon.

After about three months, a newspaper reporter contacted us to find out what we were offering on the full moon at a brand-new community centre. The interview appeared in the local newspaper, and we found it a little confronting at first. The journalist had written on the front page, "A group of women doing strange ceremonies on the full moon?" What strange ceremonies? Truth was, we were offering guided meditation evenings, with a beautiful table set up with flowers and food to celebrate and honour the full moon and Mother Earth. How quickly this planet has changed! That was 1996, thankfully now it is not a strange idea to honour the earth and full moon.

We thought no one would come, as our attendance had just been growing by word of mouth. We were pleasantly surprised! After the newspaper article, forty-five women arrived at the door for our next community full-moon gathering! You never know what magic the universe will gift you. Our word of mouth was not going to get those numbers of people overnight, so we had gratitude for that response we received.

The following month two men, Branden and Carl, came to our full-moon meeting and were interested in joining us. We were happy to include them, as it was never closed to men. Branden, a spiritual teacher interested in alternative energy sources and UFO's, invited my sister and me to a spiritual gathering network which met fortnightly and had started meetings around the same time as we.

We discovered a network of like-minded people open to share or learn about New Age information or alternative healing therapies, like Reiki and Sekhem healing, crystals, numerology, astrology, homoeopathy, Agnihotra Hindu ritual, metaphysical and esoteric philosophies, vibrational healers, spiritual drawing artists, UFO information, and psychic readers. A New Age shop owner who had opened a new business joined too, and we supported guest speakers from other regions.

It was a place to share passions, to help others evolve. Starting with about 200 curious people who came after seeing a small advertisement in the back pages of the local newspaper, our group grew to many more members by word of mouth. It was an exciting time in our small regional community, as so many people wanted to share and learn. New Age information was not readily available or found easily, but I'm pleased to say now you can find alternative therapies readily available in healing centres everywhere in main-stream communities.

I was surprised to find the leader of the Spiritual Gathering network to be Nigel, previously my real estate agent who'd sold me a vacant block of land five years prior. I asked him how the gathering began. Nigel shared that he was in the Himalayas, trekking toward base camp in Nepal, when he had the inspiration and calling to go home to Australia and start a spiritual network so no one would feel alone, and to bring all the community groups together. It was his passion to bring like-minded people together to share. His leadership style was heart-centred, relaxed and friendly. Nigel was gentle, free-flowing, and inclusive of everyone, and was very well liked. I remember his favourite saying at gatherings, "We are all one, let's share."

The gatherings were rich with information and workshops, I found so much to learn in esoteric knowledge and became the editor of the news magazine that was produced to encourage everyone to share their wisdom. So many synchronicities and meaningful relationships came from that gathering network. It became a social and spiritual community, with events being offered and some romantic partnerships developing between members. It filled my heart to be part of the community and fed me with optimism for the new world, in which we now live.

Do you ask questions without being stuck on finding the answers?

I never stopped asking questions, and never got stuck trying to find the answers. Each day I thought, *let's see what unfolds.* I looked for the joyful callings and kept exploring.

I joined a group in Sydney learning about the ancient earth wisdoms in mystery schools. We learned past-life regression therapy and third-eye activations, and channelled Egyptian masters of the past who shared messages with us about the earth changes to come. Exciting times! All the learning made me feel so passionate and alive! Memories from past lives flowed and I learned how we forget our past lives when we reincarnate back to earth. We are still living with outdated superstition and beliefs on this earth. Some people still believe we are a solid mass, and separate from everything. This thinking has been changing, with quantum science proving we part of a unified field of intelligence of vibrating energy.

My spiritual journey was becoming immensely exciting, exploring with like-minded people encouraging more questions on the universe and the eternal question of how do I fit in here? I started to receive many messages for myself, visions and insights that gave me guidance in my life. I was remembering more of Who I Am and why I reincarnated on earth this time.

I continued without any plan. I just flowed with whatever my heart and soul guided me to, and I noticed at every turn that doors were opening for me to step in and try a new experience — and a new teacher would show up for me.

Have you ever found an opportunity to help others on this earth? How did it happen for you? If yes, how did you feel afterwards?

I had an opportunity to support Mother Earth by organising a World Peace Event. The Spiritual Network gathering was gaining momentum and growing with every month's newsletter. I felt passionate about a world event coming up, called Spring Equinox World Peace Meditation Event in 1996. The details were coming from my groups in Sydney who were gearing up for this big world event. I felt in my heart to do this locally where I lived, not go to Sydney, which was 100 kilometres away. Nigel and I had similar callings to support a more loving world, so I invited him to join me on the project, as he had a good-sized network, leaving me space to network in other regions.

The event was to occur at 8 p.m. in different time zones across the planet, for twenty-four hours. This would give Mother Earth acupuncture of love across her body, the planet. So many people came forward to offer assistance with networking and the logistics on the night. It all felt so magical and easy. My sister was keen to deliver the meditation session for the world and her husband set up the sound system.

We sought permission from the local park authorities, and to our surprise 400-plus people came to the top of a beautiful mountain at a regional location that night to meditate, play musical instruments and sing in the biggest circle I had ever experienced. The power of love from the group was so palpable, we all felt it. We charged $1 for the candles sold, which paid for our venue hire to the government authority. It worked perfectly, the universe provided exactly the money we needed so no one was out of pocket.

We held it on the mountain, outside under the stars, with a mud-brick building to offer tea and coffee, and for networking afterwards. We had no idea at the time, but later found out it was a sacred Aboriginal site with a birthing cave for the women nearby, and another cave down the hill for men to do ceremonies. On the night, two Aboriginal men turned up after playing their didgeridoo in a cave nearby. They had heard us and wanted to know what was happening, then decided to share their music with us.

There were so many stories and synchronicities of how people found the event. Someone was in an elevator and heard two people talking about the event, another guy driving past saw a sign at the bottom of the mountain and arrived with his didgeridoo and played beautifully. We were asked if another would be offered, so we planned another gathering on the same mountain for Summer Solstice, three months later in December. Offered as a picnic day for families to be involved, we included an earth ceremony. It was very successful with all the families.

That was the first of many magical experiences. My heart felt incredibly warm and happy to be part of such a huge event for the time, and so many wanting to be involved made it joyful and easy as a community. We all felt it was a huge success, with so much joy being generated from everyone wanting to take part in this event, they talked about it for months. Nigel and I both realised that night that we could work really well together. For me, the event was another confirmation that when we work from our soul's calling for a higher purpose we are supported by the universe to make it happen joyfully and with ease.

Have you ever seen the connection between your inner self and the outer world?

I started to see that this connection between my outer world, my inner world, and the universe was moving things around when magic and miracles were happening.

One year had passed and it was Nigel's birthday week. We were both separated from our partners, they had moved on and we were single again. Nigel invited me to dinner as friends, and spoke on a more personal level than previously. We had no idea how much we had in common, with our passions and travel experiences across the planet.

This was the beginning of an extraordinary romantic partnership. We have enjoyed twenty-two years of travelling across Australia and the world together, connecting with Mother Earth with profound conscious travel experiences with expanded hearts. We have been shown so much magic from Mother Earth.

I have always felt that the universe moved things around and our souls guided us to one another for some extraordinary events to take place to support Mother Earth. We felt we were together for a higher purpose, more than we knew at that time.

Have you ever made a drum or played in a drum circle group? What was it like for you? If not, would you like to try it?

"Heart drums" for me and Nigel were born at our first workshop together as new partners. We joined an American Indian Medicine drum-making weekend, offered by a shamanic teacher friend from our spiritual gathering network. What a beautiful start to our relationship. Our hearts called us to take part in the weekend, we could not ignore it. Over two days we consciously connected to our drum hides and frames in meditation with visions from our drum's spirit. We did rituals and received messages on the purpose of each drum, ending with a joyful ceremony singing and chanting with a group of beautiful souls.

Our drums share a purpose. My drum represents joy and Nigel's attracts community — no surprises there! And that is what we observed on our travels — the joy and community they bought to us when we played them. Even though they were born from the same cow hide, our messages were unique to each of us.

Since that weekend those drums have served Mother Earth in our many group circles all over Australia, shared joyfully from the heart in songs and rhythm. All the people we have met have also felt the joy and healing of the heart when they joined our circles. We could never have imagined how much joy and heart-opening those drums could have given us and others on our many journeys together. Sometimes we just play together at a campsite and observe how people come to join us, maybe just sitting with us listening to the rhythms, or keen to join us in singing or playing an instrument. I also take my treasured Aboriginal clap sticks, and Nigel has a beautiful traditionally made and painted didgeridoo that was gifted to him. He may not agree with me saying this, but he cannot play so well, however on our journeys many Aboriginal men have enjoyed playing his didgeridoo and always ask, "Where did you get this?"

I love this, a beautiful American Indian saying I once heard:

"The Great Spirit loved the drum so much he gave everyone a heartbeat."

Philosophy from Elders of the Navajo Tribe

Our higher purpose presented to us that weekend and continued to unfold on our life travels.

19

A UFO?

*Have you had contact with your spirit guides?
If so, did you find them helpful?*

My contact experiences with spiritual beings started in the 1990s. I met regularly with the ten members from the spiritual gathering network who formed the healing sub-group and used vibrational healings to help one another evolve. We received a channelled message to start using Reiki or Sekhem and were guided from our spirit guides on the day as to what would be required. It would be different each week and unique for each of us to receive the healings.

One person would channel the message and one person would lie on the massage table, while the remainder held the space over them with our hands, being guided what to do. These were powerful experiences of healing and I remember going home feeling so joyful with an expanded heart. We received many messages on humanities' part in the evolution of Mother Earth, past, present and future.

Have you ever had contact with beings from other realms of existence, or UFOs?
If so, how did you find that contact? Did you receive any messages?

On my first contact with beings from other realms I was surprised by how familiar they felt. Our group was arriving at my friend Kylie's home for our weekly meditation gathering and channelling. The house felt different, as if it were humming. I noted Kylie was a little excited, but I also felt some nervousness from her. When I asked, she replied, "In the past few days I have had cupboards opening and closing, objects I put down ending up in other rooms, when I know I had not moved them at all. The dog has been going crazy, barking and running around, so excited."

We all just listened without judging or making any comments as she explained the strange things that had been happening at her home. Then we set up our circle and tuned into the space together, while she offered to lead the group into meditation. Each week we took turns for the lead role to facilitate and hold the group space, as we believed this kept us protected and connected spiritually to go on our journeys.

As Kylie guided us into the meditation journey, I noticed how quickly we all went into the deep meditation space and shifted realities faster than previously. I felt myself leaving my body, and everyone else with me, as we moved up to the roof. A staircase came down for us to walk up, leading to a big opening inside a space vessel that was so large I couldn't see how big it was, except that it appeared much larger than the house boundary. It was very bright with light, and we were guided up the stairs to meet some beautiful beings. There was no fear and I could see the whole group with me.

We ascended the stairs to go into the large opening. I could see many tall beings dressed in white with so much light around them it was like a force-field of divine blissful love all around and beyond them. I felt it before we even met. They were waiting for us and smiling, but I noted no one was using language, they communicated telepathically. I could read their thoughts and I am sure they could read mine. The message I picked up from their minds was, "We are your star family, do you not remember us?"

"Yes, I feel your hearts to be familiar to me." My heart was vibrating blissfully in a way I had not felt on earth in this life. I cried and cried with tears of joy and felt so much love from them all. Their telepathic response was, "We are from your home star system Andromeda, beyond the central sun. We are so honoured to meet with you again."

Oh my God! This was blowing my mind; some vague memory was arising of where I had come from before this incarnation. I picked up on more of the telepathic message, "You will be back with us soon, when your mission is done here on earth, dearest one."

We were all taken to different parts of the ship, like a tour. It was amazing, with lots of lights and beings moving around gracefully. They were all very bright and full of light, tall with blue eyes. I remember being guided back down the opening, down the ramp, and returning to my body where I sat meditating in Kylie's house. It had been one hour since we had begun that experience of meeting those loving, compassionate beings.

Kylie brought us out of our deep meditation state and we were quiet, as no one could speak. Someone did say, "That was an awesome meditation, I shifted to another dimension." I could not hold back. I started to cry with joy and said, "I have never felt love like that on this earth and I did not want to come back."

Wham! The flood gates opened, everyone in the group started to share all at once. Their personal stories were identical to mine — we were all taken onto a spaceship above the house where we met with our star families. It was obviously in another dimension, as we could not see it physically above Kylie's house, but we could feel the energy humming and vibrating and see it with our spiritual eyes in another state of consciousness.

The same story was told by us all of very tall, fair beings who wore white, and the love emanating from them was not of this world. It was unbelievable to feel this extraordinary love toward me again after not feeling it at that intensity for so long in my earthly life.

Some weeks later, Kylie spontaneously injured her back and needed a walking stick. She visited the doctor, who ordered X-rays and asked if she had been in a car accident as her spine was so out of alignment. She had not, and could not explain what had happened. At thirty-eight years old Kylie needed to use a walking stick as the degeneration of her spine was quite debilitating. The doctor ordered regular physiotherapy sessions.

Arriving home one day, she felt to call on the beings from the UFO ship for help. They were very keen to help and instructed her to rest in her bedroom every day at a certain time. She did this for one week, and then the beings requested she go to a spiritual site at a remote church on the central coast for more healing. She arrived at the church with her walking stick, lay down on the altar floor for half an hour as instructed, then was told to go home and rest, that they would contact her again that day. Surprised, she got up from the ground to go home with no pain and not needing that walking stick, which had become her friend. A miracle, she thought, what did they do?

Less than two weeks after becoming debilitated, Kylie was walking freely with no walking stick and felt healed — no pain. She never started the physiotherapy and returned to the doctor for a check-up two weeks later to find her spine showed no degeneration, it was totally healed. The doctor was confused and said it was impossible, how could she have repaired herself that quickly, with such a high level of damage? She could not explain, and the doctor said in jest, "That's a miracle! You must have angels on your side." She smiled and left, and never needed to return.

We all continued to connect with the spiritual beings on the UFO ship and received guidance to do earth-healing work over the next few months. Then the ship left as quickly as it had arrived. We felt the change in her house, so did not need her to tell us. Kylie moved interstate with a new partner she married, and we received guidance to move on to new journeys and new places on the earth. I went to Western Australia with my new partner, Nigel. What great work that spiritual network did, bringing us all together to evolve more consciously and make a difference on this planet.

≈

Life just kept getting more and more exciting, with many unexpected moments as I moved in and out of realities. We live on many dimensions of existence and can access our other lives when we are more conscious, bringing such depth to our earthly experience. I was not sure whether to share this event in my book, for fear of ridicule and judgment, but I was guided to share, for the time is now. This memory has been inside of me for so long, and I have not shared outside the group until now. It feels freeing to do so, as it was a significant moment in my life.

Have you ever communed with other species and found learning from your furry companion?

Many experiences come to mind when I think of my interspecies communication in nature, particularly with my personal furry companions (cats and dogs). They have come into my life as guides to help me remember my earth mission, I call them my angels. I found them to be old souls who have travelled with me in past lives. I believe they encourage us to develop qualities of compassion, loyalty, strength, intuition, and our instincts. When we co-exist with the animals, we support growth of the emotional body and raise our consciousness. My whole life since childhood has been intertwined with interspecies communication and learning.

Dearest Charles he liked to be called, not Charlie. He was my personal furry companion dog who had an extraordinary life with me. He shared messages with me about our past life together in Atlantis and was by my side when I had my transformational awakening. I will not share the lengthy messages here (that's for another book), but I will share his last words to me.

Unfortunately, I was not with him when he died, however he came to tell me when he was going. He was living with my ex-partner who loved him, and he was happy. I was travelling across Australia somewhere and he came to me as I lay on my bed in the caravan. Daydreaming, I had his picture in my hand and was thinking I must get back to see him. He popped into my thoughts, then he came full power with his message. He had a big energy, that boy! He came in spirit to tell me he was leaving the planet, that our time had ended.

I was surprised by how calm I felt. I think it was because he had accepted his life ending. My ex waited one whole week to ring me and was very upset, trying to tell me. I calmed her and said, "I know he has passed over, he came and told me." She was a little taken a back but sounded more relaxed on hearing my response. This was my first telepathic communication with Charles, and some years later I received a very big message from him on a past life. This subject I will share in a later chapter.

Have you ever worked with rescued animals?
If so, what did they teach you?

I have cared for rescued wildlife, animals who have been injured and needed assistance to rehabilitate. One of my first rescues was a beautiful little ringtail possum who had been hit by a car in my area at night. He had no physical damage I could see but was in shock, which can also kill wildlife. He started to show signs of improvement in the first couple of days, then he went down quickly. I had been warned as a novice wildlife carer that this can happen with wildlife, they appear well, then they suddenly die. I gave the possum so much love and comforted him. When I found I could do no more to keep him alive and he declined quickly I felt awful.

He shared with me sometime later in spirit that he deeply appreciated all the love I gave him and not to be upset, as he experienced great love when he passed over and he was very grateful. It was so encouraging to know that we can always make a situation better, even if we cannot change it, if we just share love from the heart. Love and compassion are so helpful to all beings on this planet.

These were exciting times in my life, to be living inter-dimensionally, in and out of other realities at one time. I will add here that I was very grounded and held down a "normal" job. You cannot shift in and out of realities if you are not grounded, it could cause you to be too mentally unstable to function in your ordinary life. All the groups I joined were very grounded people with the same mission as myself, to work from their hearts to help humanity and Mother Earth evolve. We were unable to share this information in the 1990s for fear of ridicule or unfounded judgments about us. These were some of the most extraordinary times in my life, before I started to consciously travel and work with Mother Earth energetically. Such magic was presented to me.

"Good-byes are only for those who love with their eyes. Because for those who love with heart and soul there is no such thing as separation."

Rumi

20

A Force of Nature

*Have you ever felt a great expansion in your heart
that took you to a new place?*

I remember the night so joyfully; my new relationship with Nigel had just begun. Our hearts were expanded with love and romance, we felt extraordinarily alive and joyful. This led us into a new experience beyond this earth plane, into another realm of existence.

We had both travelled extensively before we met but had never experienced a shifting of realities like this before — it pulsated through my body, expanding my heart even more than I could have imagined. This was a whole new experience for both of us.

*Have you ever felt Mother Earth pulsating through your body,
in sync with your own rhythm? If yes, did it feel real for you?*

It came about because Nigel had an idea for our first weekend away together. He was excited to take me to view some glow worms in a cave, which I had never seen before. We drove several hours south to a small country town in the Southern Highlands, near the Blue Mountains National Park, south of Sydney. We stayed at a Youth Hostel and planned to do some bushwalking and explore the national park region.

On the first evening, after dark on a full moon, we wandered off down the road from the hostel to find the track to the glow worms. It was a beautiful, clear night, a very romantic walk for us lovers of the earth and nature. Our hearts were full and expanded with love for one another and the adventure we were on that weekend. We walked hand in hand along the trail, admiring the moon and commenting that it looked exceptionally bright that night.

We were aware of all sorts of noises in the bush and spotted many little animals also out in the full moon light. Rabbits, wombats, and small marsupials darted all over the place across our path, like they had a deadline to run for. Eventually we did arrive at the glow-worm cave and admired all the glowing worms on the cave's roof. It looked very cosmic, like stars in the heavens at night. I remember thinking how magical it all was, on a full moon night with someone I truly loved so deeply, and was sharing this beautiful experience with him at that time in my life (thirty-nine years old). Yes, the universe sent me a partner after all my initial fears about moving on from my previous partner. I had fallen in love again and we were going on adventures together, because it was both of our passions to travel; our hearts called us!

We left the glow worms, feeling in awe of the cave and returned along the trail through the bush toward the hostel.

On the way, a very strange experience unfolded, maybe magical would be more accurate; this is what it felt like.

I spotted a little wooden bench along the side of the trail and felt a very strong urge to sit and admire grandmother moon's beauty. It would have been halfway along the trail, and we had not seen anyone pass us. The seat was in a little opening in the forest, providing a great, expansive view in front of me, with the full moon shining down on me and the grass paddocks in the distance with cows grazing.

As I sat admiring the scenery, I closed my eyes to feel the moon beams on my being. I felt a strong urge to make a sound that came from my heart, powerful, like I had never experienced before. Then I felt palpable energy vibration building under my feet, coming from the earth. It travelled up through my legs, up into my body. My heart space kept feeling expanded. The urge became so strong I had no control as the sound burst out of my mouth. My eyes were still closed like I was meditating deeply, but this was not a chant. It was a powerful sound that filled my body with the biggest "AAAAAHHHHH!" sound I had ever experienced.

It was a powerful force of nature meeting my soul. I had no control over its intensity. It kept coming out of my mouth loud and clear, vibrating my whole being. Because I had no control, it lasted way beyond what my breath would normally permit. I wondered if it would ever stop, not that I wanted it to, it didn't scare me. It felt very deep and loving, blissful, coming from my heart space up to my throat. It all happened spontaneously;

the sound just kept coming out of my body without me doing anything.

The strength of it expanded my heart way beyond my body. I could feel the energy far beyond the romantic love I was already feeling. It felt as if I had this going through me for more than a few minutes, with no breath taken at all. I did not even feel to take a breath, it didn't feel like my throat was being used to sound, it was coming from my whole body and felt like I had shifted realities.

As I focused on the sound, in a deep trance, Nigel was patiently being present in the moment. Eyes open, Nigel observed what was going on around me, like my guardian. He was seeing something strange, and gently asked me to open my eyes as I kept bellowing the extraordinary sound from my body.

I could not believe what I was witnessing! All the little animals who had been darting around the path as we walked to the worm caves were now sitting at my feet, and many more were arriving. One that stood out was a wombat with her baby, just sitting beside me looking up at me. Rabbits on the other side of me were just taking in the sound. They were looking up at me in what seemed like adoration and loving the sound, their ears pricked up.

The animals showed no signs of being afraid of me or Nigel as they bathed in the sound. I needed to stop, even as I could see others coming out of the bush. I could not have asked for a more magical experience in my life, I felt incredibly blessed by Mother Earth. My heart was so expanded, so full of joy and compassion for those little animals and everything else in nature, and of course my partner Nigel, who was smiling at me.

As spontaneously as the sound had arrived in my body, it left, and sadly, so did all the animals. After waiting a few moments, they made their way back into the bush. The funny thing I remember is their acknowledgment of me, as they turned to look at me. I tried to do the sound consciously, but it didn't work and I could not feel that same expanded heart space when I did it alone, without Mother Earth's assistance sending it through my body.

I had never in my life made such a sound nor had such a strong sensation in my body. It felt like it came directly from Mother Earth herself. I felt as if I had been a channel for Mother Earth's energy and love. This quote is the closest to what it felt like for me:

> *"When you do things from the soul, you feel a river moving in you, a joy."*
>
> Rumi

What an extraordinary moment that was for us!

I started to think about the full-moon meditation gatherings I had been doing with my sister each month with the group of women. I wondered if those respectful gatherings to honour grandmother moon had prepared me for this event in some way?

It was a force of nature!

After that experience and the excitement we felt, doubt and fear arrived in my mind. I was questioning what Nigel must think of his new partner — a weird and strange woman who shifts realities with sounds like a howling dog? The truth was he accepted my strangeness and saw it as a magic moment, as I did, and to this day he still accepts my crazy stuff that presents spontaneously on our travels.

Talking later that night, Nigel expressed how he thought it was all very awesome. I realised at that point that I had a wonderful, accepting, compassionate new partner, and an extraordinary new life journey unfolding that could be very interesting with so much space to travel and play on our journeys.

It became the beginning of new conscious travel journeys for me, using sound and connecting with Mother Earth and nature as Nigel and I travelled across Australia and the world visiting sacred sites. I came to realise I could not force this sound, I had to be fully conscious in my expanded heart space with much love flowing, as it was the night of this event, very in love with my new partner, so it was not too challenging. I can do that ... I thought.

Have you ever found sound that lets you feel the heartbeat of Mother Earth?

Fifteen years on, I have discovered that the "AAAAAAHHHHH" sound I experienced is the resonance of the heart vibration for sound-healing therapy. That explains the power I felt and how it was healing me on a level I was unable to comprehend at the time, through my expanded heart, and the blissful state of being I experienced that night.

This was the beginning of many more journeys to come of shifting realities, as my heart expanded and opened me to feel the flow of nature and Mother Earth in my body and to commune with other species and sentient beings.

21

Unexpected Message

I was shocked at thirty-nine years old when I tested positive with a take-home pregnancy kit. It was the first time I had become pregnant in this lifetime. Fears arose — I was a single female and had only been with my new partner, Nigel, for eight weeks. How was he going to take the news? I knew we loved one another very deeply, but this could be a game changer, as it was going to change our lives dramatically.

Nigel, at forty-five years old, already had two grown daughters from a previous marriage that hadn't ended amicably, as his wife had ensured he would not have access to his daughters. I felt Nigel still had that wound to heal in his heart. We had not discussed having a family and I felt it was way too early in the relationship to be thinking about long-term plans. We were open to the flow of what will be, will be, without planning, and accepted a short or long-term partnership. As long as our hearts felt joy we would explore together.

Have you ever experienced excitement around a pregnancy, then to find it all changes into a new journey? What were those feelings you experienced?

Being a mum was not something I had considered in this life. When I shared the news with Nigel, he was very excited, over-the-moon happy, and an infectious feeling affected me in a positive sense, changing my feelings around the pregnancy. I remember thinking *he is so supportive, what a perfect father to have with me on this journey*, and I accepted the change in our journey together. My thoughts began to shift, thinking of the pregnancy as a new adventure. What an honour to support and guide a new soul into the world.

Disappointment struck when I shared our joyful news with my mother. Mum was keen to give me her opinion on the matter, saying, "You will have to have a termination, you're too old to have children now." I wasn't expecting her response, I was thinking more along the lines of, "How wonderful! I am going to have another grandchild." She already had two granddaughters and loved them very much. This was not what I needed to hear from my own mother. My joyful heart and excitement had turned into a heavy feeling, which triggered those old unhappy feelings from childhood of never feeling supported by Mum. I felt in my heart unworthy, unloved, disappointment, and deep sadness.

I guess she had not changed over the years, still consumed by fears and triggered by everything that happened around her and how it impacted her. So much fear within her. I have found it hard to really understand, but it is what it is, I need to accept her frailties.

I tried to work out what her real fear was around my pregnancy, but never did. As she has always had fears, I should not have been surprised by her comment. When I was about sixteen years old, I did make the conscious decision that I would not have children, as my freedom was a priority. This was probably seen as strange for a young woman born in 1958, as it was expected you would get married and have children; that we were here to reproduce and care for the children and home. I just knew in my heart I had to be a free spirit on this earth and travel, as my heart had other plans for me.

One of the fears I had was how my child would change my travel life. Could I embrace this new journey with a child and with a very supportive, conscious, loving partner? Mum was right in one sense; I was a little old for a first pregnancy and knew the risk factors were higher. Even so, I felt she had been insensitive in the way she offered those facts to me.

Before the pregnancy, Nigel and I had been physically training on weekends to go on a seven-day trek into the wilderness of Tasmania. The baby's expected birth date was not included in our trekking plans! However, Nigel, the eternal optimist, assured me it would be okay, we could take the baby! What was he thinking? I was not convinced that was an option, but Nigel talked me in to seeing it as another new adventure. He could sell fridges to the Eskimos, what a salesman! I did laugh.

Among the fears that arose was concern for my own health. I had just spent a few years healing my body after being burnt out from adrenal stress with chronic fatigue and was still monitoring my activity levels. I felt called to find books on yoga for pregnancy to look after my body. I had let my yoga lapse with the excitement of a new relationship, so I returned to daily yoga practice at home, a powerful experience that gave me a high awareness of the soul growing inside me.

With this new little soul now connected to me, I had many new dreams. Each dream was giving me a life with this soul from birth through all the years of development, but stopped at age seventeen. I meditated in the mornings and started to get messages from this soul.

I know this may all sound strange, but I can only tell you what I was experiencing. Something interesting happened. My partner was also getting messages and visions of this soul, so we started to compare notes. This experience was beautiful to share with my partner. Like me, he had highly developed psychic abilities. We were seeing the same soul growing up in our visualisations, but why were we seeing this soul from childhood up to seventeen years of age, then no more?

The messages came to us from the soul for three months, then the images stopped and I experienced a random spot bleed. I mentioned it to the doctor at my check-up, as I did not take it seriously, and she quickly rushed me to have an ultrasound that day. Sadly, the soul's body was not alive and functioning any longer in my womb. Strangely, I had not had any pain and felt physically healthy and well.

My female doctor insisted I go to hospital for a dilatation and curette procedure to remove any remnants and prevent infection. I felt dazed by the change of events, and my family was also saying I must go to hospital for my health. With so much fear placed on me about infections, I agreed and was rushed into hospital. I didn't give my body a chance to release naturally, I had no time to commune with my body wisdom.

The nightmare began after the operation.

I experienced spiked fevers and excruciating pain, as if I were delivering a three-kilo baby. I had seen births as a general nurse (not as a midwife) and attended my niece's births with my sister, so I knew what women do when delivering. That is what I was experiencing for many hours at home after I had been discharged from the hospital. I was rocking on the floor in great pain, unable to get comfortable as I felt spastic pain coming and going, again and again. It was a nightmare of pain, and what for? I had no baby to deliver.

I was taken to hospital and admitted for antibiotic treatment via intravenous drip due to the severe infection found in my blood tests. My friend was a homeopath, my sister a herbalist and naturopath, so I was given herbs and homeopathic drops to help reduce the severity of the infection at the same time.

Returning home, the pain was still intense. I asked Nigel to try using spiritual healing energy on me to reduce the pain level. What we experienced surprised us! A spiritual being, a guide, came into my energetic field and assured us it would pass soon, it was all part of a completion process needed for my new journey ahead.

My interpretation of this message was that I was having a big energy clearing, a release needed for me to move on to my next journey. When I look back, I feel that I had a healing from a past life event. How blessed to be helped by spiritual guides from another reality, how awesome my life was becoming, being aware of other realms of existence.

The trauma energy I held from my past life had been blocking me in this life from moving forward. Nigel and I both grieved the loss of this being not incarnating with us, here on earth. It did helped to receive a message of the bigger picture taking place and why I needed that healing.

I wondered if the sound experience at The Southern Highlands (force of nature) with the heart expansion was the first part of the healing? I do know sound is a powerful healer, and around the same time I had an indigenous didgeridoo sound healing at a Beltane Festival, known as a Gaelic Spring Day festival. I believe I was pregnant at the time but did not know it, when an Aboriginal didgeridoo player gave me a sound healing. I vaguely remember him sharing, "We do not do sound for woman if pregnant." The jury is still out as to whether it affected me. I was going to receive that healing one way or another.

We had quiet time to heal our grief and accept that the pregnancy was not meant to be. Then we felt called by Mother Earth, calling us back to our wilderness trekking adventure in Tasmania.

Have you ever experienced the disappointment of a miscarriage? If so, how did you feel about it? Did you find any healing message for yourself? Did you get any insights from my sharing?

After the trauma of our miscarriage, this event happened years later. I had been packing up my belongings to move to a new house and found a picture tucked away in my cupboard, long forgotten about. I had drawn it at a weekend woman's temple dance healing workshop, some months prior to meeting Nigel. The strange artwork of a female figure I believed was me, with a green vine from the womb winding around my body up to the heart, wrapping around the heart area. It looked restrictive around the chest. It was a powerful drawing, but I did not know how to interpret its message from my soul.

Many years later, as a trained transpersonal Art Therapist, I viewed it and could not believe what the drawing was revealing to me. A very graphic picture, my message was:

The womb trauma was stopping my heart from expanding, that is why the vine was coming from the womb space up to the heart as a restrictive vine around the heart.

It was a powerful message I had missed due to my limited knowledge and awareness at that time in my life. I so love the power of art therapy to heal, to take us beyond the mind of judgment, straight to the soul.

At the time I had drawn the picture of the vine, I received two other signs from my soul that I missed acknowledging. A clairvoyant friend had given me a psychic reading, "You have a child in your energy field, trying to make contact with you." I vividly remember my response. I dismissed the idea and laughed, "No chance of that! I am not having any babies!"

I also had a spiritual mentor from my ancient mystery school teachings share with me after class one day, "You have a child waiting to come through to you." I dismissed that insight too, "I am in a same-sex relationship, that won't be happening."

Wow, maybe a hit on the head may have worked for me at that time? I was just not listening. My logical little egoic mind kept making judgments about all these messages and I was not open to accept any other possibilities. How often have I ignored signs in my life, when my egoic mind is judging a fearful idea?

Have you had this experience of not listening to the signs from your soul? Could it have changed your life in any way?

I believe this experience was a needed healing because my past-life trauma was energetically blocking my heart to expand further. This opened me to many new journeys with my loving and supportive partner, Nigel.

The pregnancy experience changed me considerably. I began to tap into my feminine aspect more strongly, letting go of the masculine need to control through being fearful. I now feel blessed to be a female and to have had the opportunity to release old energy restricting my heart expansion.

I learned after this experience from two male spiritual teachers sharing at different times that they wished they were females, because men do not have this conscious opportunity to release toxic energy and clear their body through the womb. I thought that was a powerful statement to behold and share with women experiencing such challenges.

My yoga training has helped me understand much about this experience. I found it immensely helpful to explain what I had experienced from conception to miscarriage. I will share here for any who may also find it helpful, if it feels right in your heart.

Yogis believe that the subtle connection between the embryo cells and the soul to be incarnated happens at conception. However, the soul does not inhabit the body until the 120th day after conception, at which point the soul can influence and connect with the mother. This is often a time when a mother may visualise the child and feels to change some things in her lifestyle. These are triggered by the hormonal changes that affect the woman's metabolism and her intuition. It is thought that the subconscious gateway of the mind becomes more open to the mother, so she starts to feel new feelings and thoughts. The soul of the child may challenge the mother before the 120th day of pregnancy. However, the soul has not entered the foetus and so is not affected by the earth's electromagnetic field or by the actual mental state of the mother. The soul is still a free spirit.

On the 120th day of pregnancy, until the umbilical cord is separated at birth, the experiences of the mother become the foundation of the subconscious mind of the child. Whenever the mother changes her mind, that is passed onto the child. This gives the mother and the soul/child an interrelated relationship. The soul chooses the woman it incarnates through and the mother accepts or rejects the responsibility to birth the child. This is why the yogic tradition is to celebrate the 120th day of the pregnancy and the woman receives gifts then.

The yogic tradition recommends that women meditate often and keep themselves in uplifting environments while pregnant. The benefit of meditation is that it will keep the mother feeling harmonious while she is experiencing changes within herself and her environments. Also, it is recommended to be in the company of inspiring women, to share and receive support before the 120th day, as this can support a more developed soul to be incarnated. Meditating after the 120th day, she can affect the karmic state of the child. The child is also influenced at the time of conception if the parents are in a higher state of consciousness.

After the birth, when you cut the umbilical cord, the physical and auric separation begins for mother and child. Interesting to note, it takes about three years for the child and mother to build independent auras.

22

Other Realms

Have you ever experienced moving in and out of other realities? What happened to you?

My life shifted tremendously as I awakened consciously. I started to have interdimensional experiences within other realms of existence and beings. Life was becoming a magic carpet ride on my spiritual journey, with awesome interactions. I continued to remember my past-life memories and communicated with ancestors and spiritual guides. My dreams gave me messages for the future. I had contact with alien beings, and I had communication with other species.

We are more than this human organic bodysuit — we are energy vibrations within a unified field of existence beyond this earth and galaxy. We come as immortal souls to wear this mortal human bodysuit and learn about ourselves and the world around us, to evolve and expand our consciousness. When our organic bodysuit dies, our soul transforms into another state of consciousness and we return to the unified energy field of consciousness of love, from whence we came.

SEEKER of FREEDOM and JOY

Do you believe in reincarnation?
Do you know who you are, and what your purpose is here on earth?

Reincarnation is to be born anew into another body, after death. I know this, as I have memories of many past-life incarnations on Mother Earth. My mission in this life is to serve humanity by healing myself and inspiring others to find their own path beyond fears that challenge them, to move forward and heal their hearts to find the greater joy and love that awaits us all. We are here to evolve by raising our vibration and conscious awareness to new heights.

I am here for me, the future, and the ancestors, to support this planet to evolve into a new vibrational frequency. My mission is to support the healing of Mother Earth and assist humanity to shift to new levels of conscious awareness through love and joy. A message I received during my transformation is that humanity needs to heal and expand our hearts in resonance with Mother Earth, who is evolving into a new vibrational frequency.

Some of the personal experiences I share here are of moving in and out of other realities.

Past traumatic memories can trigger health problems.
Do you know any traumatic memories that have triggered your health issues?

In 2006, fifteen years after my father's death, I started having spontaneous anxiety attacks for no apparent reason. One moment I was happy driving my car or sitting at home, then I'd become very anxious about Nigel dying (who by this time was my husband). I felt overwhelmed, emotional, nervous, and anxious in my heart, then was overcome with tears. If this happened while I was driving, I had to stop on the side of the road, take a breath and breathe through it, all the while thinking, *what the hell is going on?* I felt totally confused by the emotions rising inside my heart and body.

Initially it was infrequent, then it progressed to almost daily. I didn't want to tell Nigel what I was experiencing in case I manifested what I was thinking — that he was going to die! Eventually I had to tell him, as I was very emotional and he was confused as to why. His response was a shrug and, "Don't be silly, I am not going anywhere. It's my birthday soon, I plan to celebrate it here on earth." He made light of my anxiety. Weeks passed and I had not improved, so we both agreed I needed to get professional help and get to the bottom of this emotional anxiety imbalance.

I remembered a work colleague's experience of anxiety attacks and how it crippled him. Unable to get on a train to go to work, he resorted to using medication. I didn't plan on being medicated, I needed to find the cause of the anxiety and why it was being triggered.

My sister had just been to a great spiritual retreat called Heartlands in Queensland for help with an issue she was experiencing. Great idea! I booked into the retreat and flew from Sydney. Such a beautiful property, run by an open-hearted couple. They provided private cabin rooms with a quiet, reflective Zen space and ensuite bathrooms, and delicious healthy food to warm the heart. I loved that we had an option to be alone or be in a group to work on our issues.

One of the owners was an artist and offered art materials to assist you to create in the reflective space. She was also a great cook! The other owner was a spiritual counsellor, who offered me a private consultation on my first morning at the retreat to discuss what I was needing. The session started by tuning in together for a few minutes, then he gave me a message from his channelling.

"Go and write a letter to your father."

I was shocked. I thought I had healed the grief. What could I write? I was there when he passed away, what else could I say?

"Think of all the things you may not have told your father and you would like to now. Don't hold back."

Well, that was a surprise!

I felt into my heart and wrote for two days. Twenty-five pages materialised, which totally amazed me. My time was spent in the cabin and sitting outdoors on the property with their family Labrador, who I called my angel, sitting beside me. Obviously he was a healer too, as his presence gave me much strength to write very easily. After two days, I returned for my second counselling session.

"How did you do?"

"Well, I wrote a twenty-five full sized A4 page letter."

"Wonderful, how would you like to release this? I know you will have a feeling on what works for you. We are having a campfire tonight for the group, would you like to join us?"

"Wow, that is perfect, I love to use fire for my rituals of releasing. Do I have to share my experience with the group?"

"No, this is your private journey and it stays with you, if that is what you wish for. We can be your witness," he offered.

I loved the retreat, such respect for each person's needs.

That night, we all arrived at the campfire and sat in circle. Everyone was chatting when the counsellor began, "Let us know what you would like us to do, and then start when you are ready."

Wow, this is wonderful, I thought, and replied, "Just be my silent witness, thank you, while I talk to myself here and intentionally release each page."

I held my letter in my hand and put it to my heart. I said a few private words of gratitude for this opportunity and for the fire, then opened the letter and read each page before I released it into the fire.

I was deep in meditative space and heard a noise coming from the group. Someone was yelling across the fire at me, "Look at your shawl, it's on fire!"

I had to jump up and take it off, then placed it on the ground and put the fire out. What was that all about? Then I remembered saying that after Dad's death I had not been able to make contact with him, and now here he was making himself known.

Later the group members shared how they felt something big was happening that night. The other message I received from the retreat experience and that night was that my anxieties were triggered because my partner was turning fifty-six — the age of my father when he passed over. Nigel's upcoming birthday had triggered my memory of Dad's death. As I write this now, I feel him around me, like he is giving me a great big hug around my shoulders. Bless you Dad.

And in case you're wondering, after that retreat I never suffered another day of anxiety attacks.

Not too long after this event I started to have interspecies communication with furry companions spiritually and felt a calling to learn more about shamanic teachings, in particular interspecies communication with animals and Mother Earth. I believe that when the student is ready the teacher appears, and that is exactly what happened to me. I found my shamanic teacher unexpectedly, and that was another journey.

This new heart opening gave me many more new experiences with Mother Earth. It was so exciting to be on the planet again after feeling so separate and alone before my transformation.

Do you remember your past lives and/or with your family and friends?
If so, have you found a message for yourself?

My past-life memories have presented to me often and at very unexpected times.

Here is a past life presented to me in meditation: I was with my father in another life and I was warned it may not be a happy experience to remember. In that life, Dad had me murdered because he was jealous of someone who did not even exist at the time. I believe we have had many past lives together, but this memory was very vivid on this day, as I sat in a jail cell waiting to be killed.

It was in medieval times. I was Dad's wife and we lived a royal life. I loved another country, France, for the language, culture, and literature. We were wealthy, so I was able to travel there often to learn more. My husband (Dad) became jealous of my travels and decided to have me legally killed. He had the right as my husband, because he believed I had been having an affair with another man.

A very real and intense memory, it was my last days in a cold, wet cell. I was thinking about him and my heart felt strong with love and sadness when this vision presented to me. You may think I would be upset, waiting in a cell to be killed. But all I could feel for this man (Dad) in that life was great compassion for his error thinking. In the scene I was madly trying to complete a letter to him before the guards came to take me out of the cell to be murdered publicly.

I could really feel all this love in my heart, as it made my heart beat physically faster in this life. That was my sign — I knew my body did not lie and showed me it was a truth, and how much I loved him and had forgiven him.

He did not believe I had no other lover. I truly just loved and enjoyed the literature and culture of France, and the people. I wanted him to know how much I loved him before I left the earth in that lifetime, thus the letter I was trying to write in a hurry. The last thing I remember in that vision was those beautiful sky-blue eyes that sparkled at me when he was smiling or winking at me in this life.

Many years later, I sit here now, thinking how interesting this life was to me, with an emphasis of trying to complete a letter unfinished in the past life with my father, then again in this life to the same soul. At least this time I was able to complete the letter. I believe it may have been a deeper healing than I had realised at the time. In shamanic traditions they believe complete healing can only place only when all the dimensions are cleared—past, present, and future.

I also had a past-life experience with my mother and sister in Egypt, a vision I received in meditation with a large quartz that had been a gift from a close friend — it had an obvious phantom pyramid inside the crystal. This vision presented my sister, mother and I as high priestesses who offered ceremonies, rituals, and initiations in the sacred temples of Egypt. We wore beautiful white gowns and head pieces with gold applications. It was a beautiful scene, I really treasured having it, and it has helped me see my mother and sister as my teachers in this life when I am feeling challenged by them.

My message was that my sister and mother have come with a contract to help me heal and open my heart and remember my own empowerment in order to grow spiritually. This past-life memory has helped me work on not being a victim and finding my own empowerment. It has been a challenging journey, as I have always found my mother and sister very powerful beings, which encouraged my early feelings of disempowerment. This has been my heart healing in this life, to feel my own self-worth. I have come to realise I am also very powerful, and the wound is healing now as I feel less challenged. As it falls away, I feel greater love for myself.

Have you ever had recurring dreams that keep coming to you? If so, did you find a hidden message?

I believe our dreams are one of many ways our soul tries to communicate with us, giving messages in symbolic form. A soul does not speak 3D language like English or any other human language, it works from a universal language, which is symbolic. That is why many ancient messages were symbolic, as they are powerful ways to speak to many beings.

I rarely have dreams that I remember, possibly because my soul gives me messages in many other ways, in nature or sometimes in meditation. However, if I do have a dream and I remember it, or if it is recurring, usually it's significant for me to work on what it symbolises for me.

One of my recurring dreams with a message had me in a container in the ocean with a group of people I didn't recognise. The ten of us were floating around in the deep blue ocean. I felt we had been saved from a catastrophe on the planet, it may have been Atlantis when it sank. I say this because I have had many past-life memories of Atlantis. Anyway, the container was watertight, like a shipping container with a porthole, so we could see the sky and the surface of the ocean. The vessel was large enough for us to sit or lie down or move around. We had no idea where we were floating to in the ocean, but we appeared to be trusting the journey as we bumped around in the swell. We all seemed to know one another.

This dream kept appearing to me over twelve months, then one day I had a realisation — I did know those people! I had met all ten of them at the spiritual gathering network after moving to my new home on the central coast. I had really resonated with them, as they were the ten people most committed to growing the spiritual network community, a sub-group of members I had joined. Once I realised this, we met more often to do healing practices and regular deep meditation circles together. We had some alien encounters with a spaceship while in our meditation circle at my friend's house, receiving many messages and guidance to heal the earth in our region.

Those people were part of my soul family before we all incarnated to earth. It all started to make so much sense! Once this insight came to me the dream never appeared again. I had found the purpose of my connection with the ten. We had all known one another in past lives and were together for a certain amount of time to assist humanity and Mother Earth.

Have you ever had a past-life memory present to you unexpectedly?

Past-life memories can present spontaneously! I was having a massage with a therapist I visited regularly and sharing how upset I was to read a newspaper article on people designing children with particular characteristics, such as a child with blue eyes, dark hair, fair skin, or dark skin. I guess you would call it genetic engineering. The therapist agreed it did not feel right to be interfering with the natural selection of human traits. It raised a strong reaction in her heart as a future problem for the human race just as it had for me.

As the massage continued, conversation ceased and I went into a beautiful meditative state. I spontaneously received a vision of me as a gorgeous young woman, maybe eighteen years old, dressed in a lovely white robe and looking very attractive, tall, with fair hair and skin and pale blue eyes. I was in a beautiful garden courtyard, surrounded by white buildings that appeared to be temples of some sort. Standing with me were other young women around the same age, and we all looked the same. There were also young men dressed in white gowns and of a similar age.

We all seemed to have the same type of characteristics — fair eyes, fair hair and complexion. Some of us were attracted to one another, I could feel that love in my body. We were very upset, discussing something we had been told that day. At first, I could not quite get the gist of the discussion, then I heard enough to understand. Apparently, a spiritual leader had shared with us that we could not reproduce any children, we were all sterile because we had been designed as an experiment. This was so sad, as we had fallen in love and wanted to have children. I understood why that newspaper article I read in this life upset me so much.

As soon as I received that message the vision stopped and the massage came to a natural end. I shared what a deep massage it was and the vision I had. She asked what happened, but before I finished telling her the details of the vision, she said, "Oh my God! I was in that garden with you, we were in Atlantis before the fall. You do not need to share more; I was there, too." I thought it was Atlantis, but I had not shared that, and there she was telling me my vision after massaging me.

My message from that experience was that our past-life memories are real and have an impact on this life, and can be triggered at a subconscious level in this incarnation.

I realised too that we cannot make judgments on anything in life, as we may not have all the details available to us at the time. Our triggers can be coming from a past-life event.

I don't believe we need to go looking for past-life memories, but if you are open and consciously awake a memory may present and give you guidance for healing or wisdom around a past event, assisting you to make changes in this life.

23

My Ancestors

There are so many ways to receive guidance from the soul, such as meditation, dreams in a symbolic form if you can decipher them, synchronicities that happen with someone you meet, or it can be as simple as a book falling off a shelf in front of you. I believe they are all signs of our soul trying to give us guidance, but you need to be awake and listening with all the senses to receive them.

Life has shown me there are many amazing experiences you can have on this planet when you live a multi-dimensional life, that is, if we heal our hearts we can expand our energy field to have greater experiences.

Have you ever found a connection to a current health problem from a past-life agreement?

How have my past lives affected my health in this life? My past-life memories often pop up unexpectedly when I need clarity, and I have worked with a professional past-life therapist. I have passed the doubting stage and accept what I receive as my truth, and I have received benefits on so many occasions.

I remember an event that landed me in hospital with heart pain. An anomaly was found when doctors assessed me, although I had no history of heart problems or high blood pressure. Five years earlier I had been made aware of my mother's heart condition and high blood pressure, as she had collapsed when we were at a restaurant and was rushed by an Intensive Care ambulance to an Accident and Emergency unit. The doctor checking Mum's X-ray asked if I knew she had a heart condition. "No," I replied with surprise. Apparently, Mum had been taking medication for this condition but omitted to tell her daughter, the registered nurse with experience in cardiac-care nursing! The secret life of my mother.

Five years later I, too, was in hospital with heart problems. I had been enjoying a weekend intensive yoga workshop at a beautiful retreat location, and on the last day felt a very powerful emotional release from my heart. It made me feel very sensitive and emotional enough to cry, without knowing why. We had been doing exercises around our heart space that triggered a childhood feeling, without any story detail.

Two weeks later, I was at a dance workshop working with Gestalt therapy and authentic dance to release blocked emotions, when my childhood triggers of feeling disempowered and unworthy started to rise. Later that week, I was at home practicing for a dance and art therapy workshop but had persistent chest pain and had to sit down. This happened over three days and I kept ignoring it, as it was not normal cardiac pain from what I knew from nursing. My pain was in my right arm and back area and I felt pressure in the general chest area.

After three days I was at my regular yoga class again and we worked on the heart space. I became emotional, but felt good after releasing and drove off to my next destination. The pain returned, and my intuition said, go to the clinic and see a doctor. I drove to a clinic where a nurse friend was happy to fit me in for an ECG also known as EKG.

She rushed into the doctor with the results. He knew me, and told me to go to the hospital for tests right now, asking if someone could pick me up. I was told not to drive myself. I insisted I be shown the ECG(EKG), as I could read it. It looked very abnormal, with ectopic beats all over and rhythm problems. I had left-bundle branch block in my heart (a delay or blockage of electrical impulses to the left side of the heart, which can interfere with the circulatory system pumping).

Kim took me to hospital and I was admitted for tests. I refused to have any invasive tests unless the doctors could convince me it would make a difference to my diagnosis. The rhythm settled, and I was discharged to have further tests and be monitored.

I shared a Facebook post, saying I had gone into hospital for tests on my heart, which surprised my friends as they all knew me as very healthy. One friend, Debbie Smartt, privately messaged to ask what was happening, and would I like to do some inter-dimensional healing with her around the problem? I had not considered that, but thought it a gift. Knowing her as a beautiful, compassionate person, well known in the U.S. for her great work as an Inter-dimensional Past-Life Therapist, I felt into my heart and agreed maybe there was some other issue going on that I needed to know about. (Debbie Smartt's healing modality has been advocated by other famous spiritual healers in USA.)

This quantum vibrational energetic healing was not new for me, as I had done past-life therapy many years prior of a different nature with great messages and results. Debbie took me into a deep meditation process where I accessed so much information — from my past life and beyond into other dimensions — with the emphasis on my heart problem. This became very enlightening, as I accessed a very old contract I'd had with Mum in another time and dimension.

The message I received was that I had agreed to take on her karma. What was I thinking? How incredible is that? Why did I do it? I had felt so protective of Mum all my life, since childhood, whether she wanted me to or not. I felt responsible for her. Our connection was stronger than I had realised. This contract needed to be released immediately, as it was not serving her or me any longer. I released it and have had no further issues with my heart. However, I will have a medical check-up in two years, as suggested by the Cardiac Specialist to monitor if any new anomalies appear.

It was a revelation for me to access this memory from a past life and to find the contract with my mother so I could release it. This therapy was a way to remove karmic contracts we make with others in past lives, from our soul's energetic memory body. I felt blessed to have the message transmitted to me. It was another confirmation to me of the importance of acknowledging our multi-dimensional life here on earth.

DEBRA A. LANSDOWNE

Have you ever experienced past-life memories?
If so, did you feel it in your body when you healed it?

The indigenous tribes understand and honour the ancestors and our past lives; they believe we are the ancestors of the past, present and future and that healing practice needs to be multi-dimensional. This has become my truth, based on my own experiences of meditation. You may ask, how is this past present and future possible? If you go into deep meditative state and be totally present you can access your past and future whilst, being present in time. In indigenous cultures and yogic traditions they believe we live in many dimensions energetically when on earth always connected to our past, present and future. Consider, we may be living in circular time, not in linear timelines?

Another memory, my painful shoulder, triggered a past-life memory that I needed to heal. This healing happened when I was at a shamanic workshop facilitated by two Celtic shamans who travelled the world teaching ancient Celtic wisdom. It was the time of the winter Solstice, June here in the southern hemisphere, and we were given a message that our meeting would be to energetically clear some pain of our ancestral lineages in Australia, as we have many immigrants.

Emotions arose of isolation, loss of community and family, and not belonging because they were in an unfamiliar land far from the countries in which they had lived. They felt they were aliens in Australia. There were twenty of us, and our families had come from many cultures. We were told we were gathering for a celebration on the solstice for four days; we had no idea we would be doing such deep healing work in the time together using ritual and ceremony. From my experiences in spiritual healing with groups, we often do not know why we are called together until we meet and the bigger purpose is given to us as a message at the event day.

I had arrived with a painful right shoulder; it had been niggling at me for a few weeks after spontaneously turning up. Before this gathering event, I had visited a doctor because it caused me so much discomfort. His diagnosis was the beginning of arthritis! I was only in my late forties, what would I be like by sixty? He suggested medication, which I declined. I decided to see how it was after the fun of the solstice weekend.

We did deep meditation journeys on the property, connecting with Mother Earth, nature and the trees. On the last day I could still feel my shoulder. Everyone was advanced enough to go on our own journeys without needing much guidance. During one of the outside meditation journeys I felt myself leave my body and walk toward one of the big trees nearby. I arrived at a door that appeared in the trunk, where an odd-shaped knot could be seen in the tree.

I went inside the trunk into a very big, dark, space or dimension that led to the top of a set of stairs that seemed to go down into the earth. A small dwarfish being carrying a lamp, greeted me by my name. I thought that's strange, how does he know my name? He took my hand and we descended the stairs to the lower level. We were walking along the roots of the tree, which looked more like tunnels to me. I felt excited to see where we were going, surrounded by lots of green growth on the walls. The ground below was earthy and smelled fresh.

I could see a light in the distance, a village with little lights everywhere and lots of little beings. Some looked like dwarfs, but there were other species of mixed features. Everyone seemed very busy. The houses were like little hobbit homes, that is the closest description I can offer. These beings welcomed me by name and shared they had been expecting me. We chatted for some time and they gave me messages on my earthly journey and my connection with Mother Earth. They shared they were the middle-earth people, and many above do not know they exist.

They asked if I remembered our existence from many times ago, and living in another dimensional realm, as I had been and lived there before. They sure did know a lot about me. I was sad to leave at the end of our meeting, for I loved their company. I was taken by the little dwarf with the lamp back up the stairway and shown the door out. I landed in front of the tree once more and went back into my body, sitting on the grass meditating with everyone else. I woke full of excitement to share my adventure with the group. What a magical solstice event!

Another day our group did a deep meditation healing journey to clear the karma for our family lineages in Australia. The pain in my shoulder was worse than before. During the meditation I was spontaneously shown a past-life vision of me as a tribal leader in Africa. I was lying on the ground with all my tribe around me and appeared to be dying from a severe wound to the right shoulder — exactly where the pain was. The tribe was doing a ceremony honouring my passing to the next life.

When I looked at myself, I saw a huge infected wound in the right shoulder where I had been injured by another tribal warrior. It looked very painful. My tribe was singing me and watching me die. Then I left my body and came back to the sitting space I was meditating from when the group started. The Celtic shaman offered to do a healing with me, which I accepted. My shoulder pain disappeared over the next two days and I never felt it again.

To me, that was another example of past-life memories presenting in order to be healed in this life. You need to be expanded in consciousness and to surrender to access past life visions. Shamanic journeys can be helpful if it is a past memory or trauma you need to heal.

Have your ancestors come to visit you in this life, to support you? What do you remember of their visit?

I have had many experiences with ancestors visiting me in this life. Granddad (Dad's father) presented at the Women's Healing ceremony. I remember Granddad, even though I was only four years old when he passed away. My memory of him was one of great joy, as he listened to my banter on his big bed, cuddling me as I watched him struggle for every breath. He always managed to find a smile. His dis-ease was the same Alpha-1 Antitrypsin deficiency that my father and his brother inherited. I felt close to Granddad and my grandmother; we visited them often as they lived nearby.

One day we visited and his bed was empty. My visits changed, he was not there to talk and laugh with me anymore. I was confused, where he had gone without me? I'm not sure, perhaps I was told he had gone to heaven, but what does that mean to a child? I guess I did not understand grief at such a young age.

One night when I was twelve years old, I was crying and shared with Mum that I missed Granddad, because I could feel him around me. Mum tried to console me by saying, "He's long gone Debbie, he died many years ago when you were little."

"I know, but he is here now." I knew he was with me, I could feel his energy. I got over being upset that night and could not feel him again.

Some years later, as a young adult, I attended a women's healing workshop. We were instructed to ask for an ancestor to join us for the healing ceremony circle. In my spiritual eyes, Granddad appeared to me almost immediately and took my hand into the circle of ancestors. I knew it was him, I could feel his loving energy once again. He was my guide for the ceremony. I felt incredibly excited and supported by him on that healing day, a beautiful memory of how my ancestor is supporting me in this life, in another dimension, and is with me at every turn, watching over me.

I believe children have such strong intuitive abilities because they do not have all the judgments that adults have accumulated over many years. I feel we need to encourage our children to listen and act on this sixth sense of intuition so they can feel supported and kept safe.

Another healing was given by my Grandpop (Mum's father). Grandpop was the one with the broken English accent, he was Croatian and lived on a large farm full of delicious vegetables that he sold at the Sydney markets. He lived near beautiful beaches that we would visit sometimes after helping to pick vegetables. Mostly I remember how much fun it was to explore his land with all the bushland and the yummy fresh produce we took home. I loved those visits, but sadly he passed away not long after having his legs amputated when I was in my early twenties.

Many years after he passed, I was experiencing one of my extreme headaches, unable to tolerate food or light. I'd had it for five days, an unusually long time for me. It was hideous, as I could not get out of bed to do anything. I was in my darkened room, exhausted and depressed from the pain, lying in bed in a half asleep/half awake state after drinking loads of camomile tea to relax my body. I called out to my spiritual guides in desperation, "Please come and help me release this pain," when spontaneously Grandpop appeared before me in spirit.

As I watched, he walked around me using an energetic healing technique. I felt him touch my head, then with his hands in the air above my head he did some movements I had not seen before, similar to Reiki energy healing. I lay very still until he finished. I felt so much love around me, and it felt so soothing, calmed my body, and reduced the intensity of the pain. He handed me what I thought was a gift. I was trying to see it, but could not, when suddenly I heard a loud voice in my room — it was my husband coming to check on me. I lost the connection and Grandpop disappeared. I tried to reconnect to the vision, with no success. My logical mind of striving had cut me off.

I was quite upset with my husband and blamed him for not being able to receive the elusive gift, because of his noisy entry to the room. Later, I forgave him, for he did not know what I had been experiencing, he was only trying to check that I was okay.

Soon after, I needed to go to the bathroom. In the light, my husband pointed out an area on my temple that looked strangely raised. Curious, in the mirror I saw two veins at my temple area raised above my skin, in the definite shape of a cross formation. I had never seen any veins in my temple like that before.

Over the next hour, as the headache lost its intensity, so did the protrusions on my temple. In one hour they had disappeared, and so had my headache. I felt very supported and loved by my ancestor that day.

Have you received messages from your ancestors?
Was it a helpful message?

This is a message I received from another closer ancestor to me.

I was having a massage and shared at the start of the session about the book I had started to write, questioning if I really needed to complete writing or publishing it? I was sharing my belief that many people have extraordinary experiences in their lives, why would mine need to be published?

Within seconds, the therapist said, "Your father has just come to me in spirit; he is on your right side." I started to feel goose bumps, I hadn't consciously connected with him since his death.

"What is he doing here now?" I asked.

The therapist shared my father's message, "You did not get given all those gifts and experiences to keep them for yourself; it is time to share them. Write your book, now."

That is exactly how I would have imagined him saying that to me! In spirit he sounded the same. My heart was so raw with love, he had actually made contact with me! Tears welled up in my eyes and I knew it was real. I have had so many soulful experiences and connections in my life I have grown to know that strong, soulful communication and feeling in my body when it is my truth. Wow, I better get my book written and published!

The therapist shared that she did not usually get such strong messages, but she felt his energy very strongly, and commented on my father's great sense of humour.

Have you ever felt yourself in another realm of existence and interacted with ancestors?

That is what happened to me when some Australian Aboriginal ancestors joined me in singing traditional songs. Camping in a remote area of Northern Australia, we had found a beautiful big cave to sit in to cool down from the heat of a forty-degree Celsius (104 deg Fah.) day. I felt called into the cavern and sat down on the bare ground. My heart wanted me to play my clapsticks (Aboriginal musical instruments made of wooden sticks). I had no purpose rhythm to act on, and spontaneously played an Aboriginal beat.

Quickly, I felt myself go into a meditation space and start to sing. Aboriginal sounding words came out of my mouth. I don't remember ever singing them before, but it took me into a trance. Within a few minutes I felt my reality shift and I was surrounded by many Aboriginal elder women in a large circle that filled the cave. I remember traditional food in the centre; it looked like a celebration was taking place. I could hear the women's voices as we all sang together.

Nigel, who was with me, felt he had to leave the cave and move to the entrance when he heard me singing the Aboriginal songs. He felt the energy change in the cave to be powerful and a message for him to leave. He shared later how I was in a trance state and it sounded like women's business, like I was singing cultural songs. He was right, it was indigenous women singing cultural songs. Later he told me what he envisioned in spirit: that I was in such a trance I was not in this reality.

I didn't know how I could sing those songs so fluently when I did not remember ever singing them before, but I pronounced and sang with ease in the Aboriginal language and sounds. I felt so many blessings to have that encounter joyfully and spontaneously present to me. Leaving the region to camp at another location, we stopped in a little town off the highway and passed a shop selling CDs of Aboriginal music.

I told my partner Nigel I felt guided to buy one, called Aboriginal Women's Water Dreaming songs. As we played it in our vehicle while driving, I knew straight away they were the songs I was playing intuitively and singing in the cave that day, even though I had never heard them before or ever sung Aboriginal cultural songs.

My thoughts: It was a moment in time where I shifted realities and dimensions to meet the ancestors of that land. What a joy that was to experience and keep in my memory a magic moment to behold on our consciously aware travels with Mother Earth.

*Have you found ancestors waiting for you
to arrive in another land?*

I have found ancestors waiting for me on my travels in other countries. Before leaving home, I contact the ancestors of other lands or countries prior to arriving at a known sacred site. When I arrive, I can see them with my spiritual eyes, waiting to greet me and so happy I contacted them before arriving. Often, they have a message for me.

I have come to realise the ancestors are always with us and they love us to connect with them, anytime and often, so that is what I do when outside with Mother Earth, I make time to connect with earth and honour the ancestors of the land.

Our ancestors can support and help us in our lives if we acknowledge them. They can help heal the ancestral lineages we all carry within us from our past, present, and future. I received a message from Granddad (Dad's father) after I had been doing some very deep healing on myself.

Here's what he said:

*Grandfather here dearest, you are so loved,
we are all here in awe of your work and achievements.
Do you realise what you have done for your ancestors? It is such
a blessing to have your courage and love for the earth and your
family, and your commitment to this journey you are on. We are
just here holding you, dearest, we remember the challenges*

that earth can provide, especially for a sensitive, gentle heart such as yours. We honour your courage and determination to find a way back to the light, it has been a big journey of love. We commend you for the effort and for your book.

"Which grandfather is this?" I asked.

"The one you lost as a very young little girl, you remember me and my big bed? You would spend time talking with me."

"Yes," I replied, "that was a long time ago. I remember you so dearly, Granddad. Feeling all that love that you are all sending me, I miss that love here on earth."

I have found these messages from the ancestors when I heal myself so encouraging, to know they are all batting for me and to feel them supporting me. Until recently, I never really understood why they were all so happy for me. Then I found out about Generational Pattern Shifters, and I now believe I am one — those who come to earth to heal past, present and future ancestral patterns in our family's lineage.

We all have soul ancestral groups and families, but not everyone comes to earth to do this healing. Over recent years ancestral therapists have been noticing there is one person in a family who is usually the generational pattern-shifter healer of an ancestral lineage for past, present and future generations. This is what the shamanic traditions understand very well, as they include the ancestors in their healing practices. I also relate to the shamanic belief that we are the past, present and future ancestors in this moment.

It is a fascinating subject if you are interested, but I am no expert. I have had many experiences that allow me to see this as my truth, in line with what has been found in Western practices over these past years on ancestral connections and healing with epigenetics and DNA findings. This is not mainstream thinking here, it is ancient spiritual knowledge that is rising for quantum science to examine. I believe we are just remembering our past-life learnings.

My family broke the mould — I believe we have two generational pattern-shifters, as my sister and I both fit this type of person. There is usually only one who chooses the "path less travelled" in their family. They tend to be highly sensitive, have health crises that knock them down, usually don't want medicines, are fascinated with ancestors or indigenous cultures, feel compelled toward transformation and spiritual growth in this life, and have a sacred path they know to follow.

I guess it has been a challenge for Mum, having two daughters who fit this profile and do not fit into mainstream thinking, because she has cared deeply about what other people may think and their judgments.

Are you a generational pattern-shifter? Does that change your life?

I feel that I have been healing the disempowerment, loss of freedom, and pain and suffering that the women have felt in my family ancestry. There are many layers to ancestral healing, and lots more information is available now. If you have an interest in the subject, I suggest you research "generational pattern-shifters."

I can only speak from my own experiences, as I have no formal qualification in this area.

Do you think of calling the ancestors to help you?
Can you feel their presence around you?

I like to call the ancestors to join me in group-healing workshops I offer.

Before my workshops I invite the compassionate ancestors to join in and acknowledge the traditional custodians of the land. I invite all participants to call in their own ancestors to our workshop circles. I have found this very powerful and joyful to experience together, as we all hold the space from different realms of existence. When I close the workshop down, I give gratitude and thanks for their participation with us.

24

Child of Mother Earth

Mother Earth and I have had a strong relationship as far back as I can remember. From early childhood sitting in the garden, up to this very day, I feel her everywhere, whether I am communing with her in nature or in my room writing, and I can see her.

As I feel into my long relationship with Mother Earth, I believe she has been my friend, teacher, mother, and confidant. She has shown me God flows through her and all beings on this planet, as I have felt her support and love by her very beautiful presence.

At times I have felt my well-being out of balance, experienced through my emotions and my physical body needing healing, or my mental state overwhelmed with thoughts. When this occurs, I would begin to feel spiritually separate from myself and everything on the planet. These are the times I need to go to her and feel supported. As she heals and loves me, I feel it coming from her very essence, and within a short time I feel a balanced state of well-being return.

I remember and treasure these times, feeling her powerful presence — as if God is coming through her to help me out of some very dark moments in my life. I am reminded of the love and magic she offers us on this incredible planet when we consciously connect with her beautiful soul. These are the memories I behold as my relationship with this magnificent being of light.

Mother Earth has a much bigger story to tell, and it covers eons of time. Our civilizations have come and gone, risen and flourished, shed blood, loved, wondered, learned, and risen above karma to ascend, eventually triumphing. It would take too many books to write the history of the earth, for she was here way before humans arrived. The indigenous cultures across the world have references to people of the stars, whom I call not aliens, but Star People.

Indigenous tribes have been given much information from the Star People on astronomy and plant life, far advanced for them. They give credit to the star people; you'll find this in many paintings, rock art, and cave walls. These cultures had a strong sixth sense (intuitive abilities), enabling them to communicate with other realms of existence and other species. In Western culture our intuitive ability is not given its true value, so for many it lies dormant, and may not be acknowledged or developed in their lifetime.

Are you aware that Mother Earth is evolving into a higher vibrational resonance, due to the universe and galaxy expanding? Do you know what that means to all humans on the earth?

As Mother Earth starts to expand within her body, we need to know where we will be safe. Our intuitive qualities need to be fine-tuned for us to be in safe places. There have been messages from Mother Earth, indigenous cultures, and Star People for eons about what is to come. We are now in that future, and the previously foretold shifts and changes will occur, shaking our planet as it upgrades to a new vibration.

> *Do you know what your sixth sense/intuitive awareness is?*
> *Do you use it often?*

Children have very expanded hearts and energetic fields, with a strong conscious awareness of their sixth sense and primal instincts when they incarnate into the earth. On the road to adulthood many lose this quality as their logical mind develops in the Western culture, thus the intuitive ability is not used, not even acknowledged in many cases, and can become a dormant or lost skill.

As a child I used my intuition to help me navigate an unsafe experience. I was having one of my wonderful magical explorations with Mother Earth in a park garden, enjoying the activities of nature with the birds and insects all around me. I could feel with all my senses, observing nature moving around and listening to what they were telling me. This strong connection to Mother Nature opened me to talk with nature and the animals, and I could hear them speak to me in a silent language that I understood. I always felt safe and held by Mother Earth as I sat on her ground, exploring the wonder and feeling love and compassion in my heart for all beings.

Something happened to me that closed my heart, causing me not to trust. This traumatic event presented itself in adulthood for healing, from deep in my heart's memory. Young and innocent, I was enjoying my time outside with Mother Earth. As I sat on the grass, head down looking at the little insect world below, I felt a strange energy presence around me. I turned to look up and saw an unfamiliar person.

A very strange-looking old man had approached me and was almost standing over me. I immediately read his energy — he was trying to coax me with his words. My intuition was on alert and my heart began to race.

His energy felt very dark and heavy to me, as a child. I could hear his terrible thoughts. He wanted to hurt me, and had a stick in his hand that I think he was ready to hit me with. He grabbed my arm, and with determination I managed to wriggle free and run for my life.

I was terrified! I could read his mind, "Come here, little girl; I will get you."

I could feel his thoughts of planning to seriously hurt me, and his killing instincts saying, "You will not get away." He kept repeating it in his mind. I was running for my life, scared out of my body. I felt my heart sink into feelings of great loss and abandonment from Mother Nature and my family, as I felt all alone, with no one to help or save me.

I felt my heart fill with pain, then something happened, it felt so heavy! I could feel the suffering on this planet. It was too much, and something shut down inside me, a piece of my heart. That beautiful, warm innocent heart that trusted and felt unconditional love for everything had suddenly become heavy and untrusting. I felt so alone with no family around.

I kept running until I hid behind a small building with dense bushes and trees around it. He could not see me or find me. My heart was pounding so loudly, I thought it was almost audible. I was trying to hold my breath, my primal survival skills had kicked in. He was looking for me crazily. When he went in the opposite direction, I ran back toward my house, down the road and into the little gate. I sat on the grass in my own yard, feeling very afraid, and went all quiet.

I didn't tell my family. I don't think I even had the words at such a young age. I felt like I had been abandoned by all my nature friends and family. Where had they all gone? I could not feel them around me any longer. From this time on I realised how unsafe planet earth could be and I lost trust with anyone who was not part of my family, men in particular.

As I write this, the word "kidnap" comes to mind. As an adult, that is what I would describe it as: an attempted kidnapping with sinister thoughts. The memory was deep and only came to me recently, the pain finally surfacing from the depths of my heart. When I felt the release of this pain many tears flowed, and I remembered how after that event I became shy around strangers. There was a history here several children had been kidnapped, sexually abused, and murdered in that inner-city park suburb where I lived. I felt blessed I was not one. I was saved by listening to my intuition, gut feelings, and pounding heart.

Can you remember any traumatic events from childhood that make your heart feel heavy with grief?

Do you know what happens when we are traumatised?

As an adult now accessing childhood trauma, what I remember most are the feelings in my heart of being terrified and abandoned, more so than the actual details of the event. When I was healing this traumatic memory, I had to relive all the emotions and pain to let it go. I realised I had spent most of my life healing my heart, to find my childhood innocence, my true nature that had thrived before that traumatic event.

The healing itself felt quite extreme for me. I felt deep pain in my heart, like a pressure so powerful it bought tears to my eyes. It moved from the central area of my chest to the right side, then to my back, with intense pressure, like a stabbing feeling. It felt as if I was having some sort of heart attack. The more I wrote the memory, the more intense the pain felt. It was like a vice, I just want it turned off, but I continued to write and stay as a witness until it eventually released and I felt more comfortable.

This is an example of how trauma is experienced in our body and causes us much discomfort, so much so we try to distract ourselves from it. I wanted to get up from my desk and start eating something to distract me from the pain, but my Vipassana meditation training kept me alert to stay and be the witness to heal it, to not allow myself to be distracted and push it deep down again. I kept with it as the witness; eventually it fell away. I could not deny where that trauma memory was being held in my body. I knew I had released it by not avoiding the discomfort, rather by observing it. It was time to heal it.

My insight here:
How deeply traumas are held in our energetic field, waiting for us to heal them at the right time. Pain memories arise often, but if we are not conscious enough to understand the significance of the emotions, they may seem a little extreme at the time.

I had been triggered over the years by this fear of kidnapping, abandonment, and loss of trust, which I did not realise until later in my life. Examples are two events I experienced as a young adult when someone was trying to take me against my will — in London, and then again in Turkey. Both events triggered my childhood kidnapping experience. I remember how much fear and anxiety I felt when those events occurred. It felt more than I wanted to feel in my body at that time.

Have you ever been taken somewhere against your will and felt the danger around that person toward you? If so, how did you experience that feeling, being out of control?

I hope my story conveys the importance of why children need be listened to. They have strong guidance mechanisms and very strong intuitive powers to know when a person or situation is not safe or may cause them harm. They read the energetic field, as they are very sensitive to the energy around them with their pure expanded hearts. I believe we need to nurture and honour this quality in our children, as they are very fragile, sensitive, and need to be protected with respect for their own inner guidance. Parents, particularly in Western cultures, do not always have this strong quality so well-developed.

The most valuable part of a human being is the intuition, gut feelings. They are our antennae for life, to give guidance and keep us safe.

I believe we need to listen to our children more and respect their feelings, as they have wisdom to share with the world. Many coming to earth are very old souls like myself, who know this intuitive sixth-sense guidance very well. We need to support them to keep it strong, because sadly our culture has a tendency to make light of children's feelings (sixth sense) and disrespect that primal guidance inside of them. During childhood I was not encouraged to follow my own guidance, as I often felt controlled by my parents' demands.

Why is a child's intuition so strong? Their energetic field is expanded and clear, they have no other lessons or judgments to gauge what they feel. They feel from their primal gut instincts and hearts, and their minds are still open so they do not question what they feel, it is accepted as their truth. Children also don't have the years of trauma we have as adults, held inside us and clouding us.

Our planet is going through many changes, as many know. Our sixth-sense consciousness quality will need to be very well developed for humans to survive the changes that are upon us now and will continue over many years to come. It is so important that we nurture this quality and value its strength in each individual.

Do you have a well-developed sixth sense and gut instincts that would keep you safe? When did you last use them?

In my deep meditations over the years I have received many messages about the state of Mother Earth; I will share some of them here for the benefit of everyone.

We need to awaken to see the damage we are causing to our own survival on earth. We cannot continue to trash what sustains us with food, air, fire, and water, because it is craziness to do this to our own life-giving planet.

What can we do?

It is as simple as this:
When we start to heal ourselves we are healing Mother Earth.
As we raise our consciousness and vibration on earth, we gain insights and wisdom to see with new eyes and begin to walk with more awareness. When we become more conscious of our actions and walk in harmony and joy with Mother Earth,
we will feel the magic that starts to come to us.
This has been my experience.

Before it is too late, my soul reminds me that we are now in the eleventh hour.

Mother Earth has been warning us to listen to the warning signs —earthquakes, unpredictable weather patterns, and the ocean changing as the pole regions have started to melt quickly. The toxic waste we are producing is causing Mother Earth discomfort and she is shaking it off, releasing it to be free of the toxic discomfort. The same for us humans — when we feel discomfort in our body system we try to release it, shake it off. The earth is evolving and energetically expanding to a new vibration, as is our galaxy.

I feel the warning signs from Mother Earth as the planet changes.

Indigenous cultures have predicted these times to come and talk about listening to our own wisdom. It is time to follow our own heart, to stop following others and find your own heartbeat with Mother Earth. This is important, because our hearts are attuned to the resonance of Mother Earth's heartbeat and will guide us to where we are meant to be, as our planet will be shaking and rolling into a new vibrational resonance.

How do we stay safe?

We will need to be more vigilant than ever, watching the signs of change in Mother Nature all around us. Animals and insects instinctively tune into Mother Earth's changes, so watch them and you may start to observe their patterns of activity changing. We also need to listen to our own intuition, gut feelings, even when it is not logical guidance. Trust your inner heart compass. If you go in fear you will be confused and will not find the path to safety. Your fears will take you off course.

Indigenous cultures have been through many changes and have these stories held in their cultures. When asked what, where, and who will keep us safe, they always refer to the heart; they tell us to go to the heart and it will take you to the safe places, do not be distracted by the fears of others or your own fears. Look beyond these fears, as they will not serve you, it is just the logical mind keeping you from your own knowing and wisdom.

We already know the answers to everything, we just need to trust our intuition and let it guide us to the places we need to be. That is how we will survive these changes, by listening to our hearts and not the fear that is made up by our logical minds, or by the illusion of.

Learn to have control over and go beyond the logical mind, as it will make judgments and cause you fear based on old memories that do not serve us on this planet any longer. We now live in a new earth vibration urging us to live from the heart and soul, for this is our true compass. These are big times on the planet. To survive we need to trust our own sixth sense, consciousness intuition, and inner guidance.

Mother Earth has been through these transformational shifts many times, long before humans arrived on this planet. Some of us at this time have lived through these times of transformation in previous incarnations and know what is needed to navigate. The way is through the heart and soul of our immortal infinite spirit of existence that continuously changes and reincarnates into an organic physical body. The body is mortal, made of earth, and is left behind to be recycled by Mother Earth when we die; thus we sustain Mother Earth with our used-up body.

Mother Earth is a grand, glorious planet with great capabilities and wisdom to transform. We just need to be respectful of that and honour her for our own growth and survival.

This is not what is happening, at this time. Mother Earth is being raped, beaten, confined to her old skin.

We live in grand times on earth and should feel honoured to be here, to have the opportunity to awaken into a more evolved state of consciousness very quickly, if we so choose.

Have you noticed the signs Mother Earth has been showing us? What are some of the signs you have found?

This message came to me more recently, we are being called now to listen to the signs of change that are upon us.

We need to stop exploiting the earth — it is not acceptable to keep digging and exploiting the earth mother. It is disrespectful to be doing this. The earth has been trying to warn us that there will be repercussions if we do not stop and honour this planet, and that we are naïve to underestimate the strength of these changes coming to humanity. We will feel the repercussions causing many problems to our human bodies and to our homes. It has already started, but many are still not getting the messages the earth is sending us. People are not listening to the warnings, so it will be very uncomfortable for everyone in times to come, if not now. I foresee many innocent ones affected by the earth changes, but if we follow our heart guidance we will be in the right place at the right time to avoid the devastation, which is evident already if we see the news reports across the planet. Mother Earth cannot stay

limited any longer, she is expanding with or without humanity. We need to open our hearts to heal, or we will be part of the carnage that will continue with the expansion process.
It is the earth's destiny to be expanding at these times in life, can we not see this? Many are not listening or acknowledging this shift on the planet. It is easy if we follow our hearts; we will be guided to safety at times of wild events happening. Mother Earth is responding to humanity's disrespectful actions. We need to stop the mining, stop the explosions on the earth mother. We are damaging the planet that sustains us.

Here are two events that come to my mind that caused devastating effects some years ago. In 2010 an offshore drilling test rig called "Deep Horizon" blew up in the Gulf of Mexico, causing a massive fire to burn in the ocean and tons of oil to be released across the Gulf. The resulting devastation killed and maimed sea life and animals over hundreds of miles into the southern American coastal areas. Residents in affected areas say it is still not cleaned up and they experience the effects today.

When I saw this portrayed in a movie recently, I could feel Mother Earth's blood boiling up to the surface. I observed and felt the discomfort in my body. My thought was, She is bleeding! Stop drilling and digging her, why are they not listening to Mother Earth?

Japan's Fukushima Daiichi nuclear disaster of 2011 also caused devastating effects to the environment — on land and in the ocean. Radioactive materials from the plant continue to leak into our oceans to this day, as no one can shut it down safely. The contamination is seen by fishermen who collect deformed fish in their nets. Originally in the northern oceans, it is now travelling the ocean current system and affecting more areas.

When I tuned into my body, I felt this as acid in Mother Earth's stomach, leaking out and burning her body and ours, causing great pain and suffering for what I believe will be many years to come. I googled this and found it to be true that enriched active uranium 235 has a half-life of over 703 million years, long after we are gone.

> *If you cannot see this connection to yourself, think of where all your food and water comes from and how you breathe. This does not come from any other human, it comes from our beloved planet — Mother Earth.*

If we do not honour our earth, we will be unable to sustain ourselves. We need to honour our own bodies and the earth to change Mother Earth's resonance to a place of peace and joy. If only many more humans could understand that we need to release our fears by everyone opening our hearts so we can find more love in our life, because life is all about love. More love will expand us. Be the love, heal those hearts to be more open to the new resonance that is coming into this planet, our mother's body.

The ancestors have asked me to share this and remind people to connect with them whenever possible, and to honour Mother Earth.

> *She is our real mother who bore us and sustains us with air, fire, and water and grounds us on earth. Our physical mothers agreed*

and allowed the seed to be born within them, so we could go on our learnings and explorations of earth.
We need compassion for our physical mothers, as they are also having a human experience here on earth and are learning how to find their own path through the challenges they may encounter in life. They are doing the best they can with what they have available to them. They may not always be perfect to us, but we need to respect and love them unconditionally, as with Mother Earth.

I am given the message from my soul that it is the destiny of the earth to find peace within.

Feeling into Mother Earth is an extraordinary experience, as the earth holds the records of time on this planet and of all who have visited before now. If you can connect with Mother Earth, you will find a mirror with many things for you to know, and all the magic that nature holds. I know this, because it is exactly how I have experienced Mother Earth in my own life. With great love and gratitude Mother Earth will show you the many mysteries of life and the magic behind many things in nature.

Mother Earth will show you that there is no real time as we know it. Time is not linear — it is made up of circular time cycles going around at different frequencies. For example, the seasons change in cycles. The sun and moon have a cycle, the other planets have a connection and cycle with Mother Earth, and she has cycles of movement within this galaxy in which we live.

All that we find in the cosmos outside of this world around us is also found replicated within us in microscopic detail. So when we change on the inside, we also change what is outside of us. It is all connected, and that is what you will see when you start to heal yourself. You start to affect others around you as you have raised your personal vibrational resonance. Your vibration becomes lighter and you connect to a new frequency resonance that is a match with your own, similar to changing a radio-station frequency. Again, releasing old energy from our bodies in healing will bring about change, because we will have raised our personal vibration with the planet.

Have you noticed any signs from Mother Earth?
Did you get any new insights here from Mother Earth's message for your own safety while you are living here on this beautiful planet?

25

Biological Earth Battery

At this time, many of us are experiencing discomfort in our bodies as the planet shifts to a new vibration. Sensitives such as myself can feel the frequency changes of expansion. We also feel the effects of advanced technology passing through our bodies everywhere, such as unnatural EMF's electromagnetic fields generated by high-tension electrical wires, wiring in walls an offices, many appliances and Wi-Fi. Some people are highly sensitive and have been found to develop diseases by causing inflammation in their bodies. The World Health Organisation has acknowledged this as a widespread concern for our bodies health. There is plenty of information on the internet on EMF's, Wi-Fi causing health issues.

Have you heard of "earthing" to reduce inflammation in the body?

In 2011, when I had severe inflammation in my spine and a prolapsed vertebra, a friend suggested an old earth science using new "earthing tools to heal", more on this later in the chapter. At the time I was not able to walk more than five minutes around the block and needed to lie down flat all day for relief. The orthopaedic specialist had told me it would be a long time before I'd get some movement back and reduce the inflammation. I purchased the earthing tools that connect you to the earth and I used them. The inflammation quickly reduced, and my walking limitation increased to ten minutes, then twenty minutes. Within a few weeks I was walking an hour at a time around my suburb and I was up in the day, not lying on the floor to rest for many hours. I was back to work in six months. Extraordinary results.

I have become very sensitive to the Wi-Fi technologies — 4G and the latest that we have around us in the atmosphere now. I had noticed I was experiencing intense headaches that were getting progressively worse each week, and worse than I had ever felt in the past. I tested — I turned the Wi-Fi off all day, every day, for one week. No headaches. I have always turned my Wi-Fi off at night, but now the Wi-Fi in my home is off all day unless I absolutely need to use it. I no longer experience those intense headaches, whereas previously I had experienced two to three intense headaches weekly, and I also felt ungrounded, tired, and vague, with cloudy thinking most of the week.

When I questioned the telephone company about my in-home Wi-Fi system, I discovered an upgrade had been activated at exactly the time I started to get all my symptoms. I am happy to say I am now free of headaches if I use Wi-Fi one to two hours in the day and keep myself "earthed." I believe the Wi-Fi causes a great deal of inflammation in our bodies by interfering with our natural electrical activity. I feel it will affect any part of the body that has a weakness; for me that is my head area.

Recently, I was in a hotel with seriously strong Wi-Fi circulating around the rooms and building. On arriving, I felt a strange tension in my head as I reached the main foyer, and later started to feel nausea. It took me the first night to work out what I was feeling, then I had to check out early and leave that building. It gave me a violent headache that I only found relief from several hours after leaving the hotel, a five-star hotel chain in a major city in Australia. The chain had promoted how strong and great their Wi-Fi system was for customers on business trips. Maybe not so good when you are a sensitive!

Here's what happens when I get a headache from the inflammation in my body, particularly from Wi-Fi. Is it happening to you?

For me, the early signs of a headache approaching are a feeling of being ungrounded (like I am out of my body), vague thoughts, and difficulty thinking clearly. Next, I feel very tired, sleepy, and I need to lie down. Often pressure presents in the back of my neck and starts to build, as if my head is going to explode. Then I have a strange headache that feels like no other, maybe pins and needles in my head or a feeling of a knife going through my eye socket in one side of my face, with pressure behind it. Sometimes I feel vibration and buzzing in my head.

Lastly, I am in intense headache mode with nausea and a throbbing pain in one side of my temple, or my whole head, and on occasion my spine has felt tight and uncomfortable. When this happens, I need to lie in bed to rest in a dark room for twenty-four to forty-eight hours. I cannot use any electrical devices or read books, and all Wi-Fi technologies have to be turned off. I also need to fast, as I feel nauseated. Sometimes I can tolerate camomile, and ginger tea helps the nausea. I learned early on not to use medications, as that makes me vomit and feel worse, and the headache lasts longer.

However, if I earth myself early enough when I get the initial symptom of vagueness, the earthing practice changes the headache's intensity to be more tolerable and it passes more quickly. I also turn off or stay away from EMF's and Wi-Fi technology.

What is "earthing" and what tools do I use?
Have you ever felt that tingling sensation or a warmth under your feet when you are bare-foot on the soil, sand, or grassy field with morning dew?

Do you feel revitalized at the end of your walk? If you do, you're feeling the effects of earthing yourself and being energised from Mother Earth, which can be healing to your body.

Our Mother Earth is an alive planet with pulsating frequencies, a big biological battery that is replenished by solar radiation, lightning, and heat from deep-down in the molten core. Mother Earth's battery has a rhythmic pulsation of natural energy that flows to the surface for all beings to tap into its force. Our human design allows us to tap into this power source to energise, protect and balance our bodies.

When we have minimal contact with the earth's force, for example by wearing shoes made from synthetic material, it blocks us from the natural force to keep us healthy, so we can develop chronic inflammation in the body, causing us diseases. This has been researched extensively. If you wish to know more, Google "earthing," there is so much information available now. From the benefits I have felt from earthing myself, I believe this has become one of the most important health discoveries for me to connect with Mother Earth and heal me.

How can you earth yourself? It can be as easy as walking outside on the earth without wearing shoes, on solid ground, on sand, and immersion into water. There are many earthing tools available if you have no access to outside and need to be inside. An earth tool I use is a bedsheet with earthing properties that has fine copper wire threaded through the fabric sheet, used overnight to sleep on, the other is an earthing mat placed under my feet at the computer. There are yoga mats and mouse pads for the computer to reduce inflammation in the hands. They have all been designed to access the earth's pulsating force using a purpose design plug to connect into the earth. Apparently, some elite athletes are using earthing sheets to sleep on and believe they recover faster using them overnight when they are in big competitive events. There are now many more products available to buy on the internet, check out Earthing.

Earthing is wonderful to do when you have been on a long flight. Get outside, put your bare feet on the ground and consciously feel it. Jet lag and time zone differences will hardly affect you as your body will sync to the earth zone to which you have travelled. Go for a swim in the ocean or lie on the ground with your naked hands and feet touching the earth; this will help you balance your energetic field and reduce the inflammation that arises from all the Wi-Fi technologies around you.

Most people do not do earthing for enough hours for their bodies to stay healthy. The body has a big job trying to balance the energetic fields around us, natural or technological. When the body is given an opportunity to connect with the earth's force, it will naturally start to resonate and flow with the earth's healing pulse bio-energy.

And don't forget your animals — they also need to be energised by Mother Earth's battery.

Early in 2019, during deep meditation I asked, "As humans, how can we stay healthy with the next generation technologies that create electro-magnetic fields and 5G technology?" I received the following message:

You already know!

"Yes," I replied, "but we now have 5G. Is it more damaging to us humans?"

Keep using your body to help heal, it is all the same whatever the technology, keep earthing with your body. The earth can protect you, but you need to be bare on the belly of Mother Earth to feel and receive that healing energy. Make sure you tell others of this. It is so simple; humans all make it so complicated. It is your bare skin and feet on the earth, this will protect you. Keep bare skin as often as you can on Mother Earth, it will help you, because it is an organic bio-system. The technology around you is not organic, it will not be of benefit for your body. Keep getting closer to the earth with your bare skin, hands and feet. The time you spend with Mother Earth's battery needs to be much more than many humans are already doing.

There will be illness for people who are not connecting with the earth's organic battery. There are many other reasons why people need to be bare-footed with earth to feel the rhythmic pulse through their bodies, so don't be limited in thinking. Technology is just one reason to be connected, but all need to be connected for the many changes that are coming your way and will occur in waves across the planet.

This has been my future message to let many know of these changes, and to connect, it is so important.

I have great gratitude for this message to remind us to earth more often.

Have you heard of earthing tools or earthing yourself? If so, do you use the tools or practice this basic primal activity without tools?

26

Don't Forget the Animals

I cannot leave out the exploitation of animals and their needs on this planet. We need to stop and address this problem. Our animals are powerful; they incarnate to help and support us. Many are old souls, as I have experienced with many of my own furry friends who have known me well and try to help and support me. Harley, my cat, is a soul who has come to help me in this life. I am reminded as I write this book to find more time to listen to him.

I'll share just a few examples of the exploitation I refer to that deeply saddens my heart, making me almost sick in the stomach. In Australia we cull wild animals like wild horses and kangaroos, factory-fishing ships empty our oceans of marine life, while seismic testing in the oceans affects the annual migration pathways for whales and other species along our coastline. Meanwhile, our wildlife are being left without homes due to the devastating clear-felling of our native forests. The way we treat livestock and take their lives without honouring them makes me weep, as does the sedation of animals in parks for tourist photos and keeping them locked in confined spaces for our entertainment (such as a dolphin or a lion). So much is happening on land and ocean, begging us to think about what we support, I feel they are without a voice.

Experiencing and feeling the pain of Mother Earth in my body became a reality after my transformation and conscious awakening in 1992 when my dad passed away. I could not ignore what I felt. I would see the big holes dug for new buildings in the city and feel a hole opened in my own body. This may sound extreme to you, but this is what happens when you are a sensitive and have started to expand your heart enough to feel Mother Earth's body as your own. The separation melts away as you shift into another reality of conscious connection with all beings.

Feeling the trees began when I was communing with them; each started to feel like my family (brothers and sisters). When I witness them being cut down or disrespected, I feel the pain in my heart as though we are related. If you are forced to cut down a tree, try to honour its life by connecting with the tree's soul before you take it down. If given the chance, it can retract its energy from the roots up into the trunk above the earth. Then all the insects and birds will have an opportunity to leave the tree and look for new homes. This is not permission to remove trees, it is an honouring practice that I have found helpful and a way to honour Mother Earth. I feel such sadness to see them chopped down. I have been in ancient forests, more than 500 years old, during clear-felling. I felt the pain and tears of those beautiful souls.

All species are trying to communicate with us and can teach us to be more aware and conscious.

I believe the winged, the two-legged and the four-legged, all beings, are here with a soul just like us and have chosen to live in a bodysuit different from the human one. My experience is they have lessons and messages for us to learn more about ourselves. I have had numerous communications and messages from many species. Some indigenous and Buddhist traditions believe we return as other species, and that is one of the reasons they honour all beings.

Do you have companion animals at home? What is your relationship with them?

My own furry companions have shared messages at a soul level about my past lives with them as humans, and how they are with me now to help as spiritual teachers. My Burmese cat Harley is a great example. He came into my life twelve years ago and shared that we were in Egypt together as spiritual leaders, that I needed to start doing my yoga again and that art would help heal me in my life. I took on his message as real, returned to my yoga practice and studied art therapy. It took me on a whole new learning journey of heart openings, therefore enriching my life with more magic.

Wildlife have also communed with me at a soul level. Injured animals I have rescued may not always live, but they always have gratitude for the love that is given to them, and for being rescued. Most of all, they talk about how they felt really peaceful, and all the love around them when they passed over. They say that is the most important thing to know — to keep giving them love, even when they are dying, as it gives them a calm transition without fear.

Another species here on earth are the Stone Ones (that's what I call them) who hold many records of time. Often they have crystals inside, giving them a strong light. I have enjoyed a long connection with them from childhood. I only collect them if I feel called to, as I have learned they have families and do not want to be separated. If I feel called to take them, I ask first. Sometimes they ask to come with me. I have experienced many events with stones and crystal families, but that's another book!

We have so many opportunities to communicate with other species in nature. Sometimes I will ask an animal or a bird that has come straight to me, "Do you have a message for me today?" They will, if I am patient and my heart is fully open in the present moment.

Do you ever receive messages from Mother Earth?
If so, was the message helpful to you?

At one time I was really struggling with the painful emotions of feeling rejected and not loved by my family, and Mother Earth popped into my mind with this message:

Forgive your family, they did not know that what they were doing was causing you trauma, they did not have your foresight to see what was happening on this planet. You have superior knowledge of the planetary changes because you have been here before to help this planet. Remember Atlantis? You were there before the downfall. Do you remember this time?

Yes, I thought, for I have had some past-life memories of those previous incarnations. This understanding changed so much for me about my family challenges. It was a surprise, yet when I felt into my heart it was undoubtedly my truth, as I experienced the tingling in my body that I know so well — when my soul is telling me a truth.

Have other species come to give you a message?
If so, did it help you, and how?

Some time ago, I'd been indoors for a few days, focused on my computer, as I was busy writing. I felt the call to go outside and sit in my yard to eat my lunch, something I would normally do but hadn't for days. I sat with nature under a beautiful tree canopy and a kookaburra bird came and sat beside me on the table. He kept staring at me until I asked, "What message do you have for me today?"

The reply was, "Remember your family outside, come out and be with us, too." To be reminded of the beauty I had missed from having been inside for too long brought tears to my eyes and warmth to my heart. Message delivered, he turned his back to me and flew off into the distance. I now have all my meals under the tree canopy and the birds come to sit with me, moving around the branches foraging for seeds, or they just sit on a branch near me. I feel so blessed to experience nature in such beautiful ways where I live.

One night, while shutting the blinds before bed, I spotted the full moon's rays streaming through our big bay window, lighting up the living room. I decided to sit with the full moon energy as it beamed through and bathed me in bright light. My heart called me to play my shamanic medicine drum and sing a shamanic song to honour Grandmother Moon, while I sat watching and enjoyed her beauty.

Sitting in a bay window, twenty-five feet from ground level with tree branches almost touching the window, I drummed joyfully. A large male possum appeared on the branch opposite me, and remained as I opened the window. He appeared to be listening to me! I had an audience with another species! How joyful this was, a magic moment shared with a possum friend in my neighbourhood. The message he gave me was, "We are all outside at night and you can commune with us at any time." I soaked up the feeling of enjoying a moment with another species under the moon, and he did not leave until I stopped playing.

As I learn to be more awake, I realise that divine consciousness is in everything around me. I have experienced the universal force of love that surrounds us all, and I do not need to find it because I have awakened from my sleep time (unconscious).

Indigenous cultures have been known to call Western civilizations the "walking dead." Do you know why? Because in the west we are still seen as unconsciously walking around, not feeling the universal force of love around us. Indigenous cultures do have that connection; that is why they are so keen to save, respect and honour Mother Earth. They know they are part of her and not separate.

Some years ago, I was out in nature and very present in my heart space, feeling great joy and excitement as we cruised down the river Murray (the largest river system in Australia) on a camping safari. We were surrounded by very old gum trees and I could feel the ancestors watching me. They showed their heads of elders, across the branches in the knots, and their full bodies were out of the trees, leaning on the old gum trees along the riverbank. It was a strong vision, I could hardly believe it was real. I blinked and changed my focus, but it persisted strongly.

I checked in with the people I travelled with, convinced they must be able to see the ancestors too, but they all looked at me, confused. "No, we cannot see what you are describing." I was disappointed to be alone in experiencing the magic of seeing the ancestors, but then I felt blessed that the ancestors had shown themselves to me, which they continued to do for the whole day as we travelled many kilometres along the river.

How does this magic happen for me? When my heart is engaged it opens my energy field to be expansive to allow the experiences to present unexpectedly. I feel great love for all with gratitude and I stay totally present in that moment; then the most profound magical things spontaneously present to me. If I have expectations, that means my mind is engaged. The mind judges experiences, then interferes with my soul connection and my heart-energy expansion.

At times, I have found it painful to be on this planet, with so much suffering. It is all around us, because we believe we are separate from Mother Earth. So much healing is needed, and yet more trauma continues to be passed on to the next generation. How animals are treated is what I feel passionate about changing, and how children are innocently exploited and abused. Children do not have any way to gauge what the planet is about, only by what they experience and see around them, as I did. It is such a distorted experience, but it is how many will see it. I am optimistic that many will heal themselves, to change this planet to joy.

At times, I have felt so much I have had to close my eyes. As a child, I tried to speak up, only to be told I was being silly because it is okay to cause pain and suffering to other beings. Such a strange message for children to receive and pass on to the next generation!

I believe if we promote a joyful and peaceful planet, if we stop hurting others, we will change the future trajectory of pain and suffering that we are on.

I have heard some say the world is a place where we carry our burdens on our shoulders, such as the avatar Jesus carried the cross for our sins. I cannot subscribe to this thinking, as I believe it promotes more pain and suffering and that we are limited to being a victim, unable to change ourselves or the world.

What I have experienced is that when I heal myself, I find the pieces missing from my heart from traumatic events that happened to me. I can connect with my soul essence at a very deep level through the heart, and I begin to get a glimpse of the world outside me as being part of me. I feel the soul of a flower, tree, mountain, or river, and I commune with those souls and realise they are an extension of my own body. I have a personal body and I have an extended body, they are all part of my body.

This universal energy runs through all of us, through all beings and nature. Trees are not just trees, they are my lungs. The river is my circulation, the earth is my body, and the air my breath. The fire and passion in my heart is the fire in the stars from which I originated.

When connected to universal energy I feel the presence of spirit of everything flowing through me and I remember my true nature, that memory of wholeness returns to me and I feel healed. This means I am a conscious being, conscious of my connection with the universal force of love that surrounds us. I no longer feel separate from anything.

> *"The world is full of magic things, patiently waiting for our senses to grow sharper."*
>
> W.B. Yeats

27

My Soul Knows the Way

"You owe it to yourself to be yourself."
Yogi Bhajan

What did I leave behind, learn, and struggle with to find meaning in my life, freedom, love, and joy?

As a child I felt such pain from my heart being shut down, and suffered from not being respected or heard. I felt abused emotionally by being sent anger and other negative emotions. I felt the pain of others. I struggled to find ways to get past the pain, so I found a way; being in a fantasy relieved the discomfort that pain caused me. I felt much compassion for others when I was young and was confused, why did so many others experience so much pain? Then I started taking that pain on in my own body, not realising as a child how that would affect me later on.

As I grew older, I tried to run away from the painful experiences. When I did not feel love from my family at home, I found love in other places on earth. I started to remember my past lives with Mother Earth, that she was my real mother, and if I felt pain in my heart I would always feel nurtured when I communed with her.

I kept pushing my frustration and pain down deep into my heart. Then I started to forget the love in my heart, I started to lock people out, thinking they might get too close and cause me more pain. Mother Earth and the animals gave me a beautiful source of unconditional love; being with them I felt more love than I had found with human beings.

As a teenager, when I felt the pain I had a soul friend to share with. Jason helped me remember the love I had in my heart, and not to be afraid of sharing my heart with others. He was my angel who helped me get through challenging times as a teenager trying to make sense of this crazy world, with all the pain and suffering everywhere.

When I started to travel, I'd forget the pain from my childhood and family life of restrictions, anger and frustration. I would see only the beauty of the earth that I remembered from my past lives. I learned to trust my own gut feelings and I decided not to listen to others, as I believed I knew what was right for me.

I began to feel my heart guiding me after I started to connect with my soul, when I learned to meditate. I gained the connection I had lost and was able to feel the bliss and connection to all that is, to totally trust in my own instincts and heart calling, to allow my own wisdom to come through to show me the way to find my own answers.

I began to remember why I was here, and my past-life memories helped me see how I can help humanity. This became my total purpose and gave me greater love in my heart to feel compassion for myself and Mother Earth, how she also needs us to respect and remember her. Then my body started to feel sensitivity to Mother Earth's pain from all the exploitation that humans were doing to her.

Have you left any painful life experiences behind in your life?
Are you living from your heart or your fear?

How did I find more joy?

I followed my soul and heart's calling. This led me to joyful experiences, to open and expand my heart and mind to greater conscious awareness and more joy. So much unfolded I had not considered that I was getting heart healing without realising it was happening. I don't remember ever having any plans, I trusted that my heart and soul knew where I was going, and it was healing my heart in the most profound ways with joyful experiences with Mother Earth.

I tried to view everything in life as the curious child, wanting to explore beyond the fears of what my mind was telling me with its warnings and judgments, or what my family judged as not logical. I agreed with them, but I did what my heart was calling me to do beyond the logical mind. What I have learned is that the heart works differently from the logic of the mind. The heart is expansive and spontaneous, it connects with the divine unified field of consciousness around us. My calling never made sense to my family or me, but I did it anyway. I trusted my heart and it took me to places of joy!

I learned to go beyond my fears, because I found the resources within me to go as a child and find the magic that awaited me. I learned how my expanded consciousness brought such excitement and joy into my life. I have explored life on so many new journeys and realities. I believe being limited is so difficult, as it does not invite creativity, it limits the heart's ability to feel more love and allows the mind to control you by living in the past. When I expanded my awareness consciously, I found myself freed up — living a new life with more freedom physically and spiritually. I found freedom while living inside this human bodysuit which I had previously found very restrictive.

> *"Transcend your fear of the unknown by keeping your attention on the present moment."*
>
> *Rumi*

My insight here:
Our souls are trying to connect with us at every moment, but we often do not hear or see the messages for our growth. We can consciously connect with our soul in many ways, such as meditation, noticing synchronicities, our dreams, the arts, conscious dance movement, day dreaming as a form of meditation, or someone may share a message with us that seeds a thought for us to act on.

If we are walking as conscious beings, we will see the lessons and messages we are given at every moment in all things around us. Staying present to the moment is helpful, because it brings the past, present, and future into alignment for us to see what is truly happening within and around us.

Behind my childhood shadows were gifts for me to find — my compassion and my sensitive nature, and my strong connection with animals and Mother Earth. Before I could travel, I coped by believing I was a living Alice in Wonderland.

As a teenager and young adult, I found freedom and joy in adventures and travel. My angel friend Jason shared my sensitivity, feeling the pain on this planet, so I felt less alone. Travelling with Jason I began to feel the great joy of exploring Mother Earth; my heart and soul felt soothed from all the beauty and I would forget my painful family life. Then I explored the world alone, meeting many new souls on my travels.

During the second part of my adult life I was transformed after my father's death and my grieving. I found a new life, becoming more conscious and aware after healing my heart from the past. I had experienced deep separation, the "dark night of the soul," to be reborn into a more joyful existence. My new metaphor became "Phoenix rising from the ashes."

The transformative power of meditation and silence became a new experience to explore other realms of existence that gave my life more meaning. My experiences with Mother Earth were changing as my personal vibration shifted to a more conscious human being. I connected with my soul and the unified field of consciousness that surrounds us all. I remembered my soul's purpose on earth and my passion returned.

My epiphany at the Vipassana retreat reminded me of what bliss and being in oneness feels like on earth, which inspired me to follow my purpose. I could see the truth through the illusions on earth, and realized I must follow my own heart guidance, as that is the only truth. Time sitting with my soul in meditation gave me the space to receive my own wisdom, which empowered me to trust that I have the answers within me.

My past lives were presenting and helping me know Who I Am, and why some relationships existed, whether happy or challenging to me. My purpose to help humanity and Mother Earth was very strong, I could not ignore it as this was my only purpose and why I came here to Earth. I felt it a gift in my heart to remember and feel my compassion for Mother Earth, and I connected with other souls on my journey who were here to support Mother Earth and humanity, and that gave me more knowledge when I had forgotten.

The more I healed my heart, remembering ancient earth wisdoms, the more my vibration awareness was expanding. I started to connect with other realms of existence and commune with other species, as my body was becoming more sensitive to Mother Earth. I communed more deeply with the earth and I could feel the pain in her body. I started to see the exploitation and disrespectful acts humans were carrying out behind the mask of illusion and lies. My body began to feel the pain of all sentient beings, and Mother Earth started to give me messages to share on the state of her body, as she is expanding and needs more respect from the human race.

Feeling connected to my soul and the unified field of consciousness, I feel peace within me and I am manifesting my abundance as I need it. Joy presents at every turn, as I have travelled this planet and my own country being conscious, honouring, and feeling Mother Earth's beauty. I meet extraordinary people along the way who are doing great work to help humanity and Mother Earth. Mother Earth presents so much magic to me; I get so excited to spend time with her.

I never know what will present on my journeys, as I will shift realities to find a new experience to explore. I have been manifesting and creating whatever I need along the way, as I understand that when we are on our true path, our purpose, it all comes to us from the universe without our trying. Sometimes I receive gifts in ways I may not have considered, so I stay open to what is presented, and it is always more than I could have imagined. My heart sings being with Mother Earth with passion and purpose, and I know the ancestors support me on my journey as they often have made themselves known to me.

My heart guided me to write this book. It has been one of my biggest challenges and one of the deepest heart-healing experiences of my life. It has cracked my heart open for deeper healing than I knew could be possible. The gift is that it allows more light to enter into those very dark, cold places I had shut down. I needed to trust, and now the light is shining through the cracks to guide me on a new journey as an author, to share my inspirations.

I had to experience those old pains again to release them, to allow the light to be seen again, to be reminded of how we make our own pain and suffering if we react to emotions outwardly or suppress them inward, creating a pain-body. Rather, it is about being vigilant and conscious of our reactions.

My personal pains had shut down parts of my heart. I did not even remember some of them, they were so deep. At first when I was triggered and that pain arose to be healed, I was not aware enough to see what was needed. I cannot stress enough from my experience it is time to heal our hearts from pain and suffering. I have found great freedom and liberation, more than I could have imagined in my mind. When you heal your own heart, you will be healing your families and Mother Earth too. The ancestors have shared with me that it is such a blessing to have the courage and love to heal yourself, as it will heal your immediate family and ancestral lineages for the past, present and future generations. This has been my experience.

Have you considered sharing your life story?
When will you start your story?

What events prepared me to find life's purpose and gifts?

My relationships with family members challenged me in childhood to learn from those experiences, made me stronger, and encouraged me to follow my own internal guidance. My attachment to my father and his death was an initiation for me to evolve spiritually, raising my consciousness. The dis-eases I have endured showed me my strength and taught me to listen to my soul's messages. My mother has been my "tough love" advocate, challenging me to find my independence, strength of character, and to finally be empowered to survive on earth. My sister has challenged me to accept my shadows and supported me in healing them. Sharing her extraordinary healing knowledge and skills has also assisted me to raise my personal vibration.

I believe I chose the family I incarnated with for many lessons. I know my immediate family are souls I have travelled with in past lives, and we all agreed on contracts together. Thus I already knew them at a soul level, even though I did not remember that when I incarnated into this life. This has been revealed to me as I have raised my consciousness.

I believe that when we come to earth we have a story we agreed to tell, a role to act, as do our family members, to help us evolve. We have travelled in past lives with our family, but when we arrive on earth we do not remember until we start to become more consciously aware. The story is play-acted, and we feel challenges and limitations in our relationships with those who come to play with us, to help us to become more conscious.

As we reflect on the challenges and heal our hearts, we release the old story and open to more joy and love in our hearts, creating a new story where we play-act, feeling more compassionate.

And the cycle continues—play-act story, feel challenged or limited, reflect on the situation, heal the heart, release old story, open to more joy and love into the heart, create a new story feeling more compassion, and so the cycle goes around.

Old story play: Feel — Reflect — Release — Open — New story play.

When our soul's story contract ends, we leave the earth, hopefully more consciously evolved.

Do you have an old story you would like to recreate? If so, what is keeping you from changing it? Would it be fear in your mind?

Mother Earth has supported me to feel loved and has healed me. Whenever I spend time with her, or any of the beings she supports and cares for, I feel the joy and unconditional love from them all. Exploring her body, I find extraordinary beauty, magic, and mystery everywhere. She has shown me other realms of existence, and the ancestors have come to remind me, for they are with her and keen to support and talk with me.

The partners I have chosen in relationships have been my angels. They supported me to follow my heart without judgment and showed me great love. I moved on from each one amicably, still feeling each in my heart with love. I have never left my partners because I did not love them; it was a calling that took me on a new journey for my soul to grow.

My husband Nigel, who I met after my transformation, is the most important of the angels to cross my path. He has taught me acceptance and to trust in divine timing. He is a big light in my life and has supported me unconditionally; I feel so blessed to have him with me.

I have always trusted my heart as it guided me to many occupations and studies, even when it did not seem logical at the time to be moving on, or I was forced to change occupations. I had to accept. Each job has taught me confidence, to be empowered, to work in teams with others, to see the difference between humanitarian and corporate jobs in this world and how they impact the planet. I experienced when my ego was in control at times and it led me to unhappy places in my heart if I did not follow my guidance. When I am helping others I feel warmth in my heart and passion for the future. That is why I find community occupations the most rewarding for my heart and soul.

Have you had the blessing of children in your life? How does that make you feel?

I chose not to have my own children, and I have no regrets. I feel it is a privilege to have children, and not enough credit or support is given for raising a soul on this planet. I was blessed to have the opportunity to be part of six children's lives, in the role of aunty, from when they were babies to young adults. I was blessed to be a godmother to two of these children. The children allowed me to feel my nurturing motherly instincts, to care for them and support them (and their parents at times). Being part of their lives has given me so much joy and love in my heart, and allowed me to be with my inner child when I was with them, creating, playing games, and connecting with the earth when we were out on bushwalks, inspiring them, listening to them with respect and always having fun together. They are all adults now so I don't see them very often, but I hold them all deeply in my heart with love and feel blessed to have had the opportunity to have them in my life and be part of their lives. I wish them so many blessings as they find their own heart's guidance.

I took on the role of surrogate mother for my younger sister from a very young age. I believe that because my parents had limitations I stepped up for my sister, emotionally. She reminded me only recently how I was her voice when we were children and have been there for all the big events in her life. Her accident, marriage, supporting her at the births of two children, supporting her work and when she had challenges in her marriage. I was around to listen and be present without judgment.

I have also had the opportunity to work with many children in the school system. This allowed me to inspire a larger number of children to play, create, be heard, respected for their knowledge as wise souls, and feel supported by an adult. I also had an opportunity to assist children with special needs. While I thought I was sharing my gifts, those children gave me so many more gifts. They also taught me about the new race of evolved children arriving on earth who are going to change the world, if they are given a chance to be who they really are.

Do you know of any angels in your life who have helped you?

I have been blessed with many angels as teachers in my life — my parents, sister, husband, extended family members, ex-partners in relationships and ancestors. Many species, including my furry companions, have come to me as teachers, all my friends who became my teachers, and so many more. I have tremendous gratitude for the angels who have come to support me and to the teachers who have come to challenge me to see my hidden shadows or pain.

Have you communed with souls on the other side of the veil to help you?

The souls helping me on the other side include my father, who is an angel keeping me on track and reminding me to "write my book." My star family supports me when I ask for help, when I heal my heart I feel them around me. Some of my ancestors and guides who I have communicated with over the years, and many I still do not know but who are around me from past lives, offer support. Sometimes it feels like I have quite a tribe that travels with me. When I call them in at my workshops, I can feel them filling the room to be part of the fun journeys I offer my groups. I also feel them when I have been on my travels, spending time at sacred sites in Australia and other continents across the planet.

What do I have to share from my challenges in life?

Stay positive and be courageous when you meet challenges and know they will pass. You are stronger than you think, your emotions can help you navigate a way to find joy and return to the light.

Love and forgive everyone you meet, and don't take their actions personally. Connect with Mother Earth, animals, and nature at every opportunity to find the beauty and love they have to share with you. We are always supported by our ancestors and we have many light beings around us helping in this earthly life.

Listen to your heart, as your soulful heart knows the way to freedom and joy.

Don't listen to other people's opinions, only your own heart's. Heal your heart so you can get to the place of joy and greater love. Be committed to a purpose of helping Mother Earth and humanity. Find the courage to make changes and it will give humanity more joy and greater love.

Be love, see love, share love, and feel love in yourself.

I work on this every day and continue to heal the shadows that present in my heart. I feel somewhat closer than I was many years ago to feeling my light once again. I feel it is now beaming through the cracks in my heart and will be a powerful source some time in the future, returning me back to the great ocean of love and light consciousness we all come from.

"Be grateful for whoever comes, because each has been sent as a guide from beyond."

Rumi

28

My Heart Tells Me Every Day

*"Let yourself be silently drawn by the strange
pull of what you really love.
It will not lead you astray."*

Rumi

My life is full of passion, as I am excited to be here on Mother Earth. I have purpose because I know why I came here and Who I Am. I have optimism for the future — that humanity can heal and make the changes that are needed to support an awakened state of consciousness for our own evolution and for Mother Earth's expansion. It may not happen overnight, but it can start with us when we choose.

*Have you found freedom, love and joy in your life?
If so, how does that look and feel for you every day?*

We all have the resources within to make changes, inside and outside of us. If we can heal our own hearts to find the joy and love that awaits us, that we all so deserve to have in our lives, it will overflow to everyone we meet and the world around us. Mother Earth will feel this in her body and our future on this planet will be raised to become one of freedom, love, joy and peace with abundance for all, just as Mother Earth has been promising us — if we can heal our own hearts.

Have you lived well, with no regrets?
If not, what can you do now to change that for yourself?

"A life well lived," is what I wish to say when I leave this planet, and that I have inspired many to do the same. It has been such a blessing and privilege to have the opportunity to explore my life with my heart and soul. After a long road of challenges, hurdles, and painful experiences that I can now say I have left behind, I now experience such incredible joy, freedom, and love and am able to share my story today. I can honestly say I do not have any regrets.

Heal your heart, listen to your heart, trust your heart,
be guided by your heart.

The joy I experience from following my heart goes beyond what I could ever have imagined in my "little mind" in this life. Tremendous excitement, wonder, magic, joy, abundance, and love have come to me as I have expanded and healed my heart. I believe my heart knew the way, but my little egoic mind did not know my path. My heart has inspired me to accept the calling of my heart's journeys, while my mind followed the heart and showed me how to physically get on that journey and maintain the momentum to explore it. As I trusted and healed my heart, it took me on an extraordinary journey of experiences. I never had a plan and never needed one. I believed.

New opportunities presented to me, all I had to do was trust my heart and move beyond the fear of my little logical mind, which was foggy with judgment. When I trusted, it all kept unfolding. I started to have interspecies communication, I remembered my past lives to help me in this life, and I communed with Mother Earth. I have been kept safe even in high-risk environments on my travels, I found purpose and meaning in my life, and my passion returned to support humanity and Mother Earth's expansion. Now I can clearly feel and see deceptive and pretentious people, as I have seen through the illusion on this planet and found my own authentic life.

One of my greatest joys, after healing my heart, was to start to see the world with new eyes, curiously, without judgment. I trusted my heart's soul guidance, at which point I knew I was returning to the childhood innocence I once felt with the world. This new expansion in my heart gave me some very exciting journeys of shifting realities on this planet, and I felt the freedom and joy that had been waiting for me to return to my innocence.

The blessings I have received from this life, living from my heart, are so many. I feel nurtured and supported by Mother

Earth and my ancestors. When I commune with her a magical moment will present spontaneously; she may send me a beautiful two-legged or four-legged being with a message. She may share a message about the state of her body and what is needed to support her expansion. In the outdoors with Mother Earth I receive so many blessings, and moments where my heart expands from feeling pure joy and the excitement of what I feel with all sentient beings Mother Earth cares for and supports. She holds the mysteries of all time within her body and the ancestors from eons ago.

Sounding with Mother Earth has changed my body's vibration so I may experience what oneness is with all beings as Mother Earth's energy light comes through my body into my heart and voice. This has been very healing and expansive, giving me an opportunity to commune with other species, in other realms of existence. There is so much magic available to us here on earth if we are conscious beings.

All my joyful and magical journeys in my life have been with Mother Earth, and they become more magical the more awakened I become each year. At first, I travelled unconsciously and enjoyed my journeys from a very 3D experience with my senses, but in the past twenty-five years I have been travelling differently, after my awakening. I travel in a more conscious state of being, by honouring Mother Earth and the ancestors. If I am present to the moment and my heart is in an expanded state, an opportunity may arise to travel inter-dimensionally, and I can use my sixth sense to feel Mother Earth's heartbeat. I love to receive the messages from the ancestors of the lands I travel to; this brings me great joy and excitement to feel so loved and supported by beings in other realms.

I feel as if I have been travelling on a magic carpet over the years, moving around the planet. I just never know what will present to make my heart sing and open to more expansion. Travelling has taught me to be in the flow of life, with no plans, to be present moment to moment.

My life is filled with freedom, love and joy, with a renewed loving connection to my family after many years. I am also connected to a community of like-minded people who share my passion for the arts, dance, yoga, and the earth. We connect to the land and nature where I live, honouring the earth in ceremony and play. These networks support and nourish me to feel loved, as we all share joyfully, working from our hearts without judgments and accepting of everyone.

I have received many gifts and magic moments from expanding my consciousness to find a world beyond the 3D reality, which has opened me to find a rich life full of passion and purpose, allowing my heart and mind to expand ever more. To be able to shift in and out of other realities gives depth to my life, to accept that I do not know the answers, that there is so much more going on around us on other frequencies that we can explore.

My intuitive ability is open and active, to see all that is not real or is unsafe for me. This expanded awareness gives me the perception to clearly see through the illusions, dishonesty, pretentiousness, and deceptions that we are all told to believe on this planet. My expanded consciousness allows me to work as a multi-dimensional being, aware of our past, present, and future all at the same time, reminding me to be fully present now, in this moment. To have memories of my many past lives is a valuable gift from the ancestors that helps me to heal and to gain insights on my soul's journey in this life, which has supported my soul's growth and expansion of consciousness to find more joy.

I believe I have created great freedom in my life because I know the 3D reality is not all of who we are, as we are the immortal soul inside the human bodysuit. I choose to have free will and not to live by all the conditions placed on us all in this 3D world. I have not lived to just work. I choose part-time work to create space to enjoy my life, and I have chosen how and when I will do that. I chose freedom from the mainstream grind of life. When I choose to work, I feel joyful because I am choosing to be at my work on my terms, and I have created and manifested what I need at that time in my life. This has meant I have to trust how it will present and be open to the way the universe delivers it. Sometimes it may not be exactly as I envisioned, but I know it is exactly what I need for my soul to grow and evolve. This has been my experience in the many locations I have lived across this beautiful earth.

The other freedom I have is not being influenced by the material world. It has very little interest to me, leaving me with not wanting things to keep me happy. I choose a simple life filled with life experiences, freedom, and joy. I know my happiness is within me, not outside of me. If I do feel unhappy outside of me, it reminds me to look inside myself to make a change.

My belief and experiences are that the universe provides everything I need in divine timing. It comes to me without competition or effort, and I have gratitude for what I have received in my life. Over many years I have experienced that abundance and money all come when I am in balance with my divine purpose, which I feel I am now working with in my life!

I am not so naïve as to believe my challenges are over; I know they can still present in new ways or at a deeper level for me to heal. The difference now is that I practice flowing between the challenges and happy moments. I practice not getting stuck on the emotion by reacting or controlling — rather, I allow it to pass as I witness. I know now that everything is in flux on this earth and everything passes and falls away, nothing stays the same.

I have also learned that a silent mind is more important than a positive mind that can take you to illusion. The silent mind keeps us from judgments and supports equanimity, which stops the cycle of pain and suffering so that we may find freedom and liberation.

Every day I leave space in my morning for gratitude and meditation, to commune with the greater infinite force that surrounds us all. This clears my subconscious mind and keeps me plugged into my higher guidance, giving me clarity in life and filling my heart with optimism and passion. I also enjoy time to tune into my own body wisdom through my yoga practice. I find this gives me a sense of my mind, body, and soul all moving together in synchronicity, which brings peace and helps my heart feel open to give and receive love during my day.

Feeling blessed everyday as I acknowledge the angels and teachers who have come into my life to support me to evolve, particularly those times when I feel challenged and they appear when I open my eyes. Such an awesome life if we can see the angels and teachers and have gratitude for them coming to us.

Unconditional love I receive from my husband Nigel and I feel towards him is a blessing everyday in my life. The adventures and joyful moments could not have been as exciting or extraordinary without him in my life. We continue to explore this planet together with great respect and love for Mother Earth consciously awakened. My other blessing of unconditional love is my furry companion Harley a sixteen-year-old wise older cat, who found me when he was four years old. Harley keeps me in line as he demands I get off this computer, telling me I need to have a break. My interspecies communications with him has been a blessing.

So many blessings and magic I have received and continue to receive. I have gratitude every day for my life and all that has been sent my way.

And this is how I experience my life: with Freedom, Love, and Joy.

This new level of expanded conscious awareness, I now find myself walking with my ancestors, Mother Earth and other souls along the way. I continue to raise my consciousness and live a multidimensional life that I believe will lead me back to the great ocean of Love and Light of pure consciousness.

Through our hearts we become one with divine love, the force unseen. Felt strongly in the heart, it is the unified field of consciousness that moves in and around us all and everything in our world, universes, galaxies and beyond. Each day I feel my magic carpet ride has only just begun, as the freedom and joy, continues with many extraordinary experiences beyond this reality.

I do hope you have enjoyed my sharing, that it has inspired you in some way to heal your own heart and feel the joy you deserve in life. Or maybe write your own book.

I look forward to meeting you again in my next book.

There is so much freedom, love, and joy available to us on earth when we awaken. When you follow your heart's calling and trust, you will manifest with the universe all that you need in divine timing. This has been my earthly experience.

Debra A. Lansdowne

References

Brainy Quotes, Carl Jung Quotes, Retrieved June 20, 2019 from https://www.brainyquote.com/quotes/carl_jung_146686

Goodreads, Shahida Arabe >Quotes >Quotable Quote, Retrieved June 30, 2019 from https://www.goodreads.com/quotes/8704164-a-child-that-s-being-abused-by-its-parents-doesn-t-stop

Goodreads, Rumi > Quotes > Quotable Quote, Retrieved August 18, 2019 from https://www.goodreads.com/quotes/103315-the-wound-is-the-place-where-the-light-enters-you

Goodreads, Rumi > Quotes > Quotable Quote, Retrieved August 18 from https://www.goodreads.com/quotes/38564-travel-brings-power-and-love-back-into-your-life

Goodreads, Rumi > Quotes > Quotable Quote, Retrieved August 18 from https://www.goodreads.com/quotes/491350-these-pains-you-feel-are-messengers-listen-to-them

Goodreads, Rumi > Quotes > Quotable Quote, Retrieved August 16 from https://www.goodreads.com/quotes/tag/rumi

Empowerment Journeys, Quantum Healing arts, Retrieved August 18, 2019 from http://empowermentjourneys.com/favoritequotes.htm

Goodreads, Rumi > Quote s> Quotable Quote, Retrieved August 18, 2019 from https://www.goodreads.com/quotes/662262-goodbyes-are-only-for-those-who-love-with-their-eyes

Upbeat Drum Circles, Retrieved August 19, 2019 from https://ubdrumcircles.com/about/videos/

Quora, Rumi (poet) > Quotes and Sayings, Retrieved June 30 from https://www.quora.com/What-are-some-famous-quotes-by-Rumi

Quote Investigator, Tracing Quotations, Tag > William Butler Yeats, Retrieved June 28 from https://quoteinvestigator.com/tag/william-butler-yeats/

Guru Dharam Singh Khalsa and Darryl O'Keeffe. 2016. *Kundalini Yoga*. London: Gaia Books Ltd.

Sage Mindfulness, Rumi's Poem The Guest House, Retrieved August 18 from http://www.sagemindfulness.com/blog/rumi-s-poem-the-guest-house

Power of Positivity, 15 Life Changing Lessons To Learn From Rumi, Retrieved August 18 from https://www.powerofpositivity.com/15-life-changing-lessons-to-learn-from-rumi/

About the Author

Debra Lansdowne is a free spirit with a passion for adventure and a relentless desire to explore our beautiful planet. A true SEEKER of FREEDOM and JOY, Debra's ability to trust and follow her heart's guidance has taken her on many journeys, where her infectious and inspiring personality and compassion for all beings helped her create lifelong friendships.

Born and raised in Sydney, Australia, Debra's strong intuition, empathy, and inner knowing made itself apparent from an early age. Debra felt tremendously challenged and misunderstood by her family during childhood, a wound she carried in her heart into adulthood. Perhaps ironically, that wound also fuelled her need to look at the world with all her senses — physically and metaphysically — with different eyes.

Leaving home at seventeen years of age to follow her heart's calling, Debra explored many paths to experience life to the fullest. A traumatic life initiation at thirty-three years of age took Debra on a new journey of discovery, to explore a new level of conscious awakening and trust her heart's guidance more courageously. In return, Debra was gifted with an extraordinary life of joy and magic that opened her mind to other realms of existence with Mother Earth and beyond the 3D world.

Debra has worn many hats in her life, all supporting others to heal themselves. First working for many years as a registered nurse, Debra then trained to be a therapist in art, counselling, conscious dance, and became a yoga teacher.

Successfully and passionately offering groups a sacred space to be inspired and joyfully heal their hearts on deep soulful journeys, Debra has now begun another new journey — as an author, sharing her extraordinary life experiences and insights.

Debra promises this book is the first of a series with insights to enlighten and inspire you to look at life a little differently.

www.ingramcontent.com/pod-product-compliance
Lightning Source LLC
Chambersburg PA
CBHW071333080526
44587CB00017B/2824